"Long live the Pope of Our Lady of Fatima!" cried out an enthusiastic pilgrim. And Pope Pius XII replied smiling: "That is what I am!"

"The most encouraging sign of the times is just this confident and ever growing orientation of souls towards the Mediatrix of all Graces; they sense that through Mary the salvation of the world will come."

(Pope Pius XII).

To the Master General of the Dominicans (1950)
"Say that the Pope's thought is contained in the Message of Fatima. Tell your Religious to continue to work with the greatest enthusiasm for the propagation of the cult of Our Lady of Fatima."

(The Pope of Our Lady of Fatima).

"It is in the **Heart of Mary** that the world will find again true fraternity; it is by the **Heart of Mary** that it will obtain pardon and mercy of God; it is with the **Heart of Mary** that the new city will be built in truth, justice and charity; it is from the **Heart of Mary**, grateful and free, will in the near future increase its manifestations of love and filial gratitude."

St. Louis Marie de Montfort.
(He is the spiritual father and inspirer of that wonderful branch of Catholic Action so widespread to-day—the *Legion of Mary*.)

More About Fatima

MORE
ABOUT FATIMA

and the Immaculate Heart of Mary

REV. FR. V. MONTES DE OCA, C.S.Sp.

Revised and Enlarged

A translation of
LE PRODIGE INOUÏ DE FATIMA
(250,000 copies)
by
REV. J. DACRUZ, C.S.Sp. (Castelbranco)

An urgent exhortation from the Virgin of Fatima urging us
to return to the full Gospel message of her Divine Son.

First Published 1945
Reprinted February 1946, April 1946, July 1946, April 1947,
January 1948, October 1948, April 1949, June 1950.
New and revised Edition 1953.
Reprinted April 1957, January 1960.
Revised and enlarged October 1971.
Reprinted September 1972.

Reprinted in Australia, September, 1974.
Reprinted in the U.S.A., April 1975.
Reprinted in the U.S.A., March 1979.

Originally published with the imprimatur
of the Most Rev. John Carroll, Archbishop of Dublin

DEDICATED
to
Pope Pius XII

who consecrated the Church and the whole human race to the Immaculate Heart of Mary, and who extended the Feast of this same loving Heart to the Universal Church.

"Let us go with confidence to the throne of grace . . ."
"In me is all hope of life and of virtue . . ."
"Thou art the *Hope* of the *World!*"

"After that, He saith . . .
                    Behold thy Mother!"

All these texts are taken from the Office and Mass of the Immaculate Heart of Mary.

CONTENTS

APPENDIX

AUTHOR'S PREFACE

Dear Reader,

This little booklet contains one of the most gripping stories you have ever come across. Read it therefore and persuade others to read it. You will find in it the authentic account by a Portuguese priest of a wonderful miracle, still quite recent, which is without any doubt one of the most stupendous in the entire history of the Church. Several learned men who were present testified: "I have seen it, but I cannot explain it." But read and judge for yourself. You will appreciate the great importance of these wonderful events which the Bishop of Fatima approved officially on October 13th, 1930.

This edition, corrected and enlarged, contains that part of the "Secret of Fatima" which Lucy has been able to reveal "with the permission of Heaven and her superiors," on the occasion of the twenty-fifth anniversary of the apparitions. It also considers the more important aspects of the wonderful events of Fatima. Its modest price aims at facilitating the clergy and those in charge of pious works, in the spreading of the important and vital message of Our Lady of Fatima among the faithful and among children and Catholic youth, with a view to arousing everywhere a renewal of the Christian life of prayer and of penance. In this way we shall appease the Divine Justice which has been angered, and thus obtain for the world the peace which is so desired.

It goes without saying that neither the fact of the apparitions of Fatima nor the messages which have accompanied them belong to the deposit of revelation proper, and that they are not truths of Faith. Similarly, the imprimatur granted to these works, whether by the Bishop of Fatima or by the Vicar General of Vatican City, does not involve in any way the infallibility of the Church. It constitutes solely the weightiest human testimony, giving us a guarantee that the official enquiry into the events of Fatima has been made in accordance with all the canonical rules, and that the facts and documents cited have been recognised as valid in law.

Rev. J. da Cruz, C.S.Sp.

PART I

THE APPARITIONS

CHAPTER I

An Unexpected Apparition
(May 13th, 1917)

On Sunday, May 13th, 1917, three children from the little hamlet of Aljustrel, in the parish of Fatima, were tending their sheep in a hollow called Cova da Iria, situated in the same parish. They were Jacinta Marto, a little girl of seven, Francis her brother, aged nine, and their cousin Lucy dos Santos, aged ten. These little mountain shepherds could neither read nor write, but being brought up in a Christian manner they could pray and had learned their catechism assiduously. Lucy had made her First Holy Communion. Their parents possessed at Cova da Iria, two miles from their home, a small piece of land on which grew some evergreen oaks.

Hearing the Angelus bell from the steeple of Fatima the three little shepherds knelt down and recited the Rosary together. After the Rosary they decided to build a "little house" which might shelter them on stormy days.

Little thinking of the symbolism of their childish actions, they chose for their fragile edifice the very spot where the majestic Basilica of Our Lady of Fatima now stands.

The little architects were thus engaged at their building when they were suddenly interrupted by a blinding flash of lightning. They looked anxiously at the sky. Not a single cloud veiled the brilliance of the midday sun. Fearing, however, that a storm might be brewing on the other side of the hill, they drove their sheep before them and hastily descended the slope. Halfway down they saw a second flash brighter even than the first. They went still faster. Then, on reaching the foot of the slope, opposite the site of the present chapel of the apparitions, they stopped, surprised and dazzled by a wonderful apparition.

13

The Beautiful Lady

Two paces away, on the foliage of an evergreen oak, they saw a "Beautiful Lady," all luminous and more resplendent than the sun. With a gesture of motherly kindness, the Apparition reassured them:

"Fear not. I shall do you no harm."

And so they remained there in ecstasy contemplating it.

The Lady is all beautiful. She seems to be from fifteen to eighteen years of age. Her dress, white as snow, tied at the neck by a gold cord, reaches down to her feet which are just visible barely touching the branches of the tree. A white veil embroidered with gold covers her head and shoulders and falls to her feet like the dress. Her hands are joined at the height of her breast in an attitude of prayer. A rosary of brilliant pearls with a silver cross hangs from her right hand. Her face, of an ineffable beauty, shines in a halo as bright as the sun, but seems to be veiled by a slight look of sorrow.

After some minutes of ecstatic silence, Lucy ventures to ask:

"Where do you come from?"

"I come from Heaven," replies the Lady.

"From Heaven! And why have you come here?"

"I have come to ask you to come here for six months in succession on the thirteenth of each month, at this same hour. In the month of October I shall tell you who I am and what I want."

"Could you tell me if the war will end soon?"

"I cannot tell you that," replies the Lady, "until I have told you what I want."

Gaining confidence Lucy continues:

"You come from heaven! What about me—shall I go to heaven?"

"Yes, you will go to heaven."

"And Jacinta?"

"Jacinta also."

"And Francis?"

The Apparition turns towards the little fellow, and looks at him with an expression of kindness and motherly reproach.

"He will go also, but he must say his Rosary."

Hearing Lucy speak about him, Francis begins to take an interest in the mysterious conversation.

"But I do not see anybody there," says he to Lucy.

Lucy in surprise then asks the Lady:

"How is it that Francis does not see you?"

"Tell him to recite the Rosary and he will see me."

Lucy does so, and Francis takes up his Rosary and begins to recite it. After six or seven *Hail Marys* he suddenly sees the "Beautiful Lady," whose brilliance dazzles him; but he does not hear her speak though his hearing is good.

Meanwhile Lucy continues to question the Apparition:

"Is little Maria das Neves, who died recently, in heaven?"

"Yes, she is in heaven."

"And Amelia?"

"She will be in Purgatory till the end of the world."[1]

Then the Lady asks them a favour:

"Would you like to offer yourselves to God to make sacrifices and to accept willingly all the sufferings it may please Him to send you, in order to make reparation for so many sins, which offend the Divine Majesty, to obtain the conversion of sinners, and to make amends for all the blasphemies and offences committed against the Immaculate Heart of Mary?"

"Yes, we should like that very much," answers Lucy in the name of all three.

With a gesture the Lady shows how much their generosity pleases her. Then she adds:

"You will soon have much to suffer, but the grace of God will help you, and give you the strength you need."

In a document of 1941 Lucy adds that on saying these words the Lady *opened her hands,* throwing on them a beam of mysterious light, at once so intense and deep that penetrating their breasts even to the inmost depths of their souls, it made them see themselves in God, more clearly than in the clearest mirror.

"Then," continues Lucy, "moved by an irresistible force, we threw ourselves on our knees, repeating fervently: 'O Most Holy Trinity, I adore You'. 'My God, I love You'."

Some moments later, the Lady *recommended them to recite the Rosary devoutly every day, to obtain peace for the world.*

---

[1] In May, 1946, Lucy confirmed that the apparition said "till the end of the world." Moreover, Amelia was by no means a scandalous Christian.

Then gliding through space without moving her feet, the Apparition departed towards the East, and disappeared in the light of the sun.

After the Apparition

Coming out of their ecstasy, the three little seers compared impressions. All three had seen. What struck them most was the motherly *kindness*, the ineffable *beauty*, of the heavenly Lady.

"Her beauty," said Lucy, "almost blinded me, and yet I did not get tired from looking at her. I should never have thought that the Blessed Virgin was so beautiful."

Jacinta had heard everything, but had not spoken. Francis had heard Lucy but not the Lady. He only learned what she said from his little companions. The apparition seemed to them to have lasted about ten minutes.

Lucy had a vague presentiment that no one would believe them, and that they might even be scolded if they related the wonderful vision they had seen. She therefore asked her companions not to tell anybody, and they promised to keep it a secret. Filled now with heavenly delight, the three little shepherds no longer had any desire to play. While watching their flock they were content to remain in silent contemplation of what they had just seen. Only Jacinta broke this prayerful silence from time to time crying:

"I see," said Lucy, "that you will tell everything."

"Oh the beautiful Lady, how beautiful she is!"

"O fear not," replied Jacinta, "I shall be able to keep the secret."

First Contradictions

But in the evening, when Mamma returned home, Jacinta ran to meet her in order to share with her the joyful news which her little heart could no longer contain.

"Mamma, I saw the Blessed Virgin to-day in the Cova da Iria."

"What! I don't believe you! Are you already a saint that you should see the Blessed Virgin?"

16

"But it is true, Mamma," persisted the little girl, somewhat abashed.

In the house Jacinta began again:

"Mamma! Francis and I are going to say the Rosary: the Blessed Virgin told us to say it."

A quarter of an hour later the child came back again:

"Mamma, we must say the Rosary every day, the Blessed Virgin wants it."

At supper, Jacinta, questioned by her mother, related in detail before the whole family the wonderful apparition. The candour of the child, her visible emotion, her exactness in the least details, and the confirmation by Francis of his sister's account, all left the parents with an intimate conviction that something mysterious had taken place. Besides, from this moment, little Jacinta became a fearless apostle in the bosom of her family. As a result of her loving insistence, she finally obtained the *daily recitation of the family Rosary*. And if work sometimes caused the prayer to be postponed, Jacinta insisted sadly: "Mamma, I have already said my Rosary, and you have not said yours." Her mother declared later under oath, before the Commission of investigation:

"In this manner had these children learnt from the apparition not only to recite the Rosary themselves, but also to make everybody recite it."

The news of this mysterious apparition was not slow in coming to the ears of Lucy's mother. Finally she questioned her daughter, who then stated the facts quite simply. The mother, clearly annoyed, was content at first with treating her as a little liar. But seeing that the rumour increased and spread everywhere, she finally became angry, struck her daughter, and wished to make her retract, and to say publicly that she had lied.

Meanwhile, the *Pastor of Fatima*, hearing everyone talking about the apparitions, asked Lucy's mother to bring her to the Presbytery. The poor peasant woman went, full of anxiety, lamenting the fact that such misfortunes should fall on her alone, and wishing to force her daughter to retract before the priest all that she had affirmed. The Pastor tried to calm the distracted mother, and then questioned Lucy. The scared child only answered shortly, and made a rather unfavourable impression. Finally, he advised the mother to allow Lucy to return to Cova da Iria, but to bring her back to him if the apparition came again.

In the village, the people ran after the three children asking them questions, but hardly anyone gave credence to their story. The majority even called them liars. As the apparition had told them, contradictions began to arise in their path everywhere. But the little seers held steadfastly to their account, and said they would return to Cova da Iria on June 13th, to obey the Lady.

CHAPTER II

The Second Apparition
(*June 13, 1917*)

WEDNESDAY, June 13th, was the feast of St. Anthony, patron of the parish of Fatima. On the previous evening, Jacinta, embracing her mother, said tenderly:

"Mamma, do not go to the feast of St. Anthony tomorrow. Come instead with us to Cova da Iria to see the Blessed Virgin."

"It is useless to go there," replies the mother, "the Blessed Virgin will not appear to you."

"O yes, yes, she said she would appear, and she will certainly do so!"

"Then you will not go to the feast of St. Anthony?"

"No! St. Anthony is not beautiful."

"How can you say that he is not beautiful!"

"This lady is much, much more beautiful! We shall go first to Cova da Iria, and if the Lady tells us to go to the feast of St. Anthony we shall go."

However, as a measure of prudence, the Marto family decided not to take part in these mysterious happenings, and on the morning of the 13th went off to the fair. The people went to the Church for the patronal feast. Only about fifty people betook themselves to Cova da Iria, most of them through curiosity.

Before midday the three children arrive. They kneel in the shade of a large oak, and recite the Rosary devoutly with the people. After the Rosary Lucy rises, arranges her clothes a little, and turns towards the East to await the beautiful Lady. The other two children demand insistently that another Rosary be recited.

Suddenly Lucy makes a gesture of surprise: "Look," she says, "that was a flash of lightning. The Lady is coming!"

She hurries with her two little cousins down to the tree of the first apparition, and the vision appears.

"Madam," says Lucy, "You have made me come here. What do you want of me?"

The heavenly vision asks them to come back on July 13th and *to recite the Rosary every day*. Then she adds:

"I want you to learn to read, in order that I may be able to tell you what I want."

Lucy intercedes for a sick person recommended to her.

"If he is converted," replies the Lady, "he will recover in the course of the year."

Continuing to speak, she confided a secret to the children, or rather "a first secret."

As Francis did not hear the words of the vision, it was Lucy who told him afterwards what concerned him. Then the Lady departed, as on the first occasion, in the direction of the East. The conversation had lasted about ten minutes.

Besides the three little seers, none of those present had seen the mysterious Lady. But several marvellous facts confirmed their impression that something extraordinary was taking place. The day was bright and hot as it usual is in Portugal in the month of June. Now, during the entire period of the apparition the light of the sun was dimmed in an exceptional manner, without any apparent cause. At the same time, the topmost branches of the tree were bent in the form of a parasol, and remained thus as if an invisible weight had come to rest upon them. Those nearest the tree heard quite distinctly Lucy's words, and also perceived in the form of an indistinct whispering, or the loud humming of a bee, the sound of the Lady's answer, alternating regularly with the girl's voice.

At the end of the apparition, there was heard near the tree, a loud report which the witnesses compared to the explosion of a rocket, and Lucy cried:

"There! She is going away."

At the same time the onlookers saw rise from the tree a beautiful white cloud which they could follow with their eyes for quite a while as it moved in the direction of the East. Further, at the Lady's departure, the upper branches of the tree, without losing the curved shape of a parasol, leaned towards the East, as if in going away the Lady's dress had trailed over them. And this double pressure which had bent the branches, first into a curve and then towards the East, was so great that the branches remained like this for long hours, and only slowly resumed their normal position.

Deeply moved by all these mysterious events, those present would willingly have remained in prayer beside the holy tree, but most of them came from a great distance away, and had to start on their homeward journey. They therefore recited the Litany of the Blessed Virgin, and departed, saying the Rosary with the children all along the way.

On passing before the church of Fatima, all these eyewitnesses, still under the influence of deep emotion, were questioned at length by those who came out from High Mass. In this way these extraordinary facts were not long in becoming known throughout the whole region.

From this day onwards, the apparitions at Cova da Iria became the invariable subject of conversation. As was to be expected, some believed, while others jeered openly, even reproaching the parents of the little seers with not recalling their children to reason.

New Trials

In face of this general excitement, the parents of the little ones were greatly perplexed. The parents of Francis and Jacinta did not doubt their children's sincerity, and in their hearts were inclined to believe in these apparitions, but how justify their convictions before the scoffers? Besides, diabolical influence was always a possibility. Then their mother in annoyance threatened one day to punish them severely if they continued to draw people to Cova da Iria. The fearless Jacinta was well able to defend herself:

"We do not call anyone to Cova da Iria," she replied. "Those who wish, go. We go ourselves, and those who do not want to go have only to remain at home! But for those who refuse to believe, the punishment of God awaits them. And be careful, Mamma, for if you yourself do not believe, God might punish you." At once the storm was averted.

But Lucy's mother was not so easily disarmed. Persuaded that her daughter was taking part in a wicked hoax, she wished her to retract publicly.

"But Mamma," replied the girl in tears, "if I have seen, how can you ask me to say I have not seen? Then I should be lying."

On being taken once more to the Pastor of Fatima who wished to question her after each apparition, she was so scared that the priest put an end to the interview with these words:

"All this does not seem to come from God, since, instead of exposing everything simply to her pastor, the child is timid and reticent. It might quite possibly be some mischief of the devil. The truth will come out in time."

The thought that she might be the plaything of the devil completed the prostration of poor Lucy who revealed her fears to her two little companions. Jacinta bravely reassured her:

"No, no," said she, "it is not the devil. The devil, according to what is said, is very ugly and lives under the earth, in hell. This Lady, on the contrary, is so beautiful, and we have seen her go up to heaven."

CHAPTER III

The Third Apparition
(*July 13th, 1917*)

JACINTA's words had revived Lucy's courage, but in the hostile atmosphere of her family, her doubts returned very quickly. On July 12th, Lucy said to her two companions:

"Do you go alone to Cova da Iria to-morrow, and if the Lady asks for me tell her that I dared not come for fear it might be the devil."

On the morning of Friday, July 13th, towards eleven o'clock, Lucy felt herself urged to go to the heavenly rendezvous. She went to the home of her two cousins whom she found in tears kneeling at the foot of the bed reciting the Rosary.

"Have you not gone yet?" she asked. "It is time to go."

"Oh!" they replied, "we had not the courage to go without you."

"Well, then, let us go together."

The parents of Francis and Jacinta followed them to be present at the apparition. Lucy's mother on the contrary remained at home on the Pastor's advice. At Cova da Iria there was already a crowd, estimated by some witnesses at from four to five thousand people. The children recited the Rosary kneeling, with the people, and the vision appeared again.

Frightened perhaps by the trials she had undergone, Lucy looked at the Lady without daring to say a word. But the fearless Jacinta, nudging her, said:

"Go on, Lucy speak! Do you not see that she is already there and that she wants you to speak?"

Thus encouraged, Lucy asked the Lady:

"What do you want of me?"

As if wishing to forestall any further hesitation, the Lady first asked the children not to fail to return on August 13th. Then she insisted, for the third time, saying:

"You must recite the Rosary every day in honour of Our Lady of the Rosary to obtain peace for the world and the end of the war for only she can obtain this."

Oppressed by the weight of her trial, Lucy asked the Lady

23

to say who she was, and *to perform a miracle* in order that all might believe in the reality of the apparitions. In similar circumstances Bernadette had begged the Virgin of Lourdes to tell her name, and to cause the briar in the grotto to bloom. But then the Immaculate Virgin had only smiled; at Fatima the apparition answered:

"Continue to come here on the thirteenth of each month, and on October 13th I shall say who I am and what I want, and I shall work a great miracle in order that all may believe."

Gaining courage, Lucy then asked her to be so kind as to cure a cripple, to convert a family of Fatima, and to take to heaven a sick person of Atouguia. The Lady answered that if she did not cure the crippled person, she would give him other means of earning a livelihood, but for that *he must recite the Rosary every day;* that the sick person should not be in a hurry to die, that she knew better than he did when she should come to take him; that the other persons' requests would be granted the following year, but that they must recite the Rosary.

At a certain moment, Lucy was heard to repeat aloud:

"Yes, she wishes people to recite the Rosary. People must recite the Rosary."

"To restore my waning fervour," Lucy adds humbly, "the apparition said once more **'Sacrifice yourselves for sinners, and say often, especially when you make sacrifices: O Jesus, it is for love of You, for the conversion of sinners, and in reparation for the offences committed against the Immaculate Heart of Mary.'** "

The Lady continued to speak, and Lucy was heard to cry: "Oh!" while her face took on an expression of great sorrow. When, after the apparition, those present wished to know the cause of this sadness, she only said:

"It is a secret."

"Good or bad?"

"For us three it is good."

"And for the rest?"

"For some it is good, for others bad."

After this secret, the apparition added in conclusion:

"When reciting the Rosary, say after each decade: **'O my Jesus, forgive us our sins, save us from the fire of Hell, lead all souls to Heaven, and help especially those who most need Your mercy.'** "

The apparition which showed itself to the three children remained all the time invisible to the rest of the crowd, as if she wished to ask of them the homage of their faith. But in order to give a basis to that act of faith, she deigned, as on June 13th, to give signs of her presence by *several extraordinary facts*.

Thus, at the Lady's arrival, all were able to see that the sun lost its brilliance, and that the atmosphere assumed a curious yellow tinge, while at the same time a beautiful white cloud enveloped the tree. Various trustworthy witnesses also declared that on July 13th they perceived once more near the tree, the whispering as it were of the Lady's voice. On the departure of the apparition a loud explosion was again heard, while Lucy cried, pointing with her finger:

"If you want to see her, look in that direction."

CHAPTER IV

The Fight Against Fatima

THE news of these extraordinary events flashed through the country, arousing curiosity everywhere.

On their side, the little seers, and Lucy in particular, became increasingly objects of contradiction. After the July apparition, Lucy's house was never without visitors who wished to see her and ask her questions, so that her mother was obliged to get someone else to tend the flock. At Cova da Iria too, the number of pilgrims increased daily, to the despair of Lucy's parents, who not only saw their own potatoes trampled, but also had to suffer the reproach of neighbouring proprietors who held them responsible for the damage caused to their crops. Naturally the family repaid Lucy for all these troubles, causing her many bitter days.

Meanwhile the ecclesiastical authority feigned ignorance of the events and held itself resolutely aloof. His Eminence the Cardinal Patriarch of Lisbon, on whom the parish of Fatima depended at this period, had even pushed prudence so far as to expressly forbid the clergy to take any part in the mysterious happenings. The Catholic Press observed on its side great reserve. If it did allude sometimes to the apparition of Fatima, it was only to recommend the greatest prudence to the faithful. Indeed, not only could the powers of darkness simulate the supernatural, but it was also to be feared that the enemies of the Church, then in power, might be just seeking to provoke these large gatherings so as to have a pretext for banning all external exercises of worship.

The Anticlerical Reaction

The enemies of the Church, on the contrary, understood almost instinctively the capital importance of the religious movement of Fatima. Since the revolution of 1910, which had driven from Portugal the King, Dom Manuel, the Freethinkers had seized power, expelled all religious from the country, oppressed the secular clergy, and were constantly persecuting the Church by impious laws, the *avowed* aim of all this being the prevention of recruiting among the clergy and the destruction of the Faith. Therefore, as soon as these prodigies of Fatima began to electrify the crowds, they felt that this religious movement threatened to ruin in a day all the work of dechristianisation that they had been doing for many years. The Grand Orient of Lisbon hastened to make its plan and to launch its attack.

The attack began with a press campaign, clearly organized, which increased steadily in virulence until the fall of the régime in 1926. The liberalist and impious newspapers began to describe at length the apparitions of Fatima, introducing circumstances both false and ridiculous in order to throw discredit on the events. According to the accounts, it was nothing but a "Jesuitical farce", a sordid exploitation of the people, a money-making affair and a plot to arouse the masses against the "Republican" government. As to the mysterious happenings reported at Fatima, they added that this was all a question of pure suggestion.

The clearest result of this mischievous campaign was to make Fatima known throughout the country and to make many decide to go and judge for themselves.

Opposition from the Civil Authority

The press campaign really prepared the ground for the official intervention of the civil authority, which was then entirely anticlerical. Fatima depended on the sub-prefecture of Ourem. The sub-prefect was Arthur d'Oliveira Santos, son of the local blacksmith, a man with but a primary school education. He directed a modest local newspaper, and had founded a "centre of Carbonari," a kind of popular free-thought group. This was enough for the Republic of 1910 to raise him, at the age of twenty-six, to the post of sub-prefect, president of the council of the department and deputy judge of the district. The accumulation of these high offices made of this half-educated tinsmith the most influential and most feared man of the region.

On Saturday, August 11th, the parents of the three little seers were cited by the sub-prefect to appear before him, at Ourem, with their children. The clever official submitted Lucy to a long examination, ordering her to reveal the Lady's "se-

27

cret" and to promise not to go any more to the place of the apparitions. When the child persisted in her refusal, he threatened the parents and sent them away saying that he knew well how to attain his purpose, even if he had to do away with these wicked good-for-nothings.

The Children are Arrested

Two days later, on August 13th, the sub-prefect could see the endless stream of people who passed his window for early morning on their way to the scene of the apparitions. Conquering his feelings of contempt, he got out of his carriage, and went to Aljustrel, to the home of the little seers.

"I have come to be present also at the apparitions," he declared. "Like Thomas, I want to see in order to believe."

"You are right," said Jacinta's father. "The best way to decide is to see for yourself."

The sub-prefect insisted on taking the children in his carriage to Cova da Iria.

"No, no," they cried, "we always go on foot."

"Well," said he to their parents, "let them go to the Pastor's house; I shall await them there to ask them a few more questions."

When the children arrived, the sub-prefect asked the Pastor to question Lucy in his presence, especially about the "secret." The Pastor, who was hearing about the secret for the first time, insisted on her telling it to him.

"The Lady has forbidden us to tell it," replied the girl, "but if you wish, I shall ask her to-day if she will allow me to tell it to the priest, and if she does, I shall tell it."

It was wisdom that spoke in the mouth of the child.

"Good," said the sub-prefect, "these are supernatural things; let us leave them aside. It is time to go to Cova da Iria."

He insisted so much on taking the children in his carriage that the parents finally yielded, and the three children entered with him, but after a few yards the clever fellow turned off in the direction of Ourem. On arriving home he tried all means to draw the secret from the children; they refused absolutely, and he locked them into a room saying that they should not leave it until they had obeyed. On the following morning an old woman came to chat with them and to try to draw the secret from them by surprise, but in vain. They were

28

then taken before the bureau of administration and submitted to a regular cross-examination. They related quite simply the story of apparitions, but declared that they could not tell the secret, because the Lady had forbidden them to do so. Tricks, promises and threats were used, but they remained inflexible.

Shortly after noon they were put into *the public prison* and told they would soon be taken out and burnt alive!

Little Jacinta, hardly seven, begins to weep. Lucy tries to encourage her:

"Jacinta, are you weeping?"

"We are going to die without embracing our parents for a last time . . . I want to see Mamma once more."

"Do not weep," begs her brother Francis, "let us offer this sacrifice for sinners." And joining his hands he says, "O Jesus, it is for love of You, and for the conversion of sinners."

Jacinta, still in tears, joins her hands in turn, and lifting her eyes to heaven adds:

"Also for the Holy Father and for the offences committed against the Immaculate Heart of Mary."

Moved by this scene, the other prisoners interpose:

"But why do you not tell the secret? What does it matter if the Lady has forbidden it?"

"O never," replied Jacinta fearlessly. "We should rather die."

Occupied as they had been, the children had not yet recited the Rosary. Jacinta then takes out a medal and asks a prisoner to hang it on a nail on the wall. Then kneeling before this improvised altar, they recite the Rosary with all their souls, while the prisoners, overcome with emotion, fall on their knees.

In the evening, the children are taken once more before the bureau of administration to undergo another searching examination interspersed with enticing promises and terrible threats.

The Threat of Death

In face of their persistent refusal, the sub-prefect has recourse to a last stratagem. He rises roughly, gets into a terrible rage and shouts:

"If you will not obey willingly, you will do so by force."

And turning towards the usher, he tells him to go and prepare a huge cauldron of boiling oil in which to roast the little rebels. While the usher has gone to carry out the order, they are shut into a little room. What moments of anguish for the three little martyrs, who prepare themselves for the sacrifice! Suddenly the door opens and the sub-prefect calls Jacinta:

"You will not tell the secret? Well, you will be burnt first. Follow me."

The little one follows him without hesitation. Led into another room, she is again questioned, caressed, threatened, and finally shut up in another room.

The sub-prefect then calls Francis:

"Your sister is already roasted. The same fate awaits you if you do not tell the secret."

Francis remains as unshakable as Jacinta whom he finally joins in the other room. After a moment it is Lucy's turn.

"And what did you think they were going to do to you?" she was asked later.

"I was convinced that he was going to kill me like my two companions, but I was not afraid, and I recommended myself to the Blessed Virgin."

Surprised at this constancy, in such young persons, the sub-prefect had them mentally examined by a doctor who found nothing abnormal.

On August 15th, the magistrate made a last attempt, but without any greater success. With a heroism evidently above their natural strength, the little seers kept faithfully the secret the Lady had confided to them. The sub-prefect, tired and disappointed, then decided to send back the three prisoners. But, perverse to the end, he took advantage of the time when the people were at High Mass to take them back secretly to the presbytery, whence he had taken them by trickery. This prejudiced the people against their Pastor whom they falsely suspected of connivance in the arrest of the innocent children.

Sectarian Counter-Manifestation

As we shall see in the next chapter, the arrest of the children did not prevent the crowd from witnessing, on Monday, August 13th, at Cova da Iria, prodigies *all the more remarkable in that they were produced in the absence of the little seers*. So the people returned home more enthusiastic than ever. Without losing time, the Free-thinkers organised for the following Sunday, August 19th, a counter-pilgrimage with all its Carbonari elements and with the full concurrence of the police under the presidency of the sub-prefect of Ourem. But on the day appointed they found Fatima only a deserted village. The whole village had gone with their Pastor to celebrate the Divine Office in a distant chapel. Thus the impious counter-manifestation was a failure, and events at Fatima continued their irresistible course.

CHAPTER V

The Frustrated Apparition
(*August 13th, 1917*)

ON MONDAY, August 13th, the newspapers estimated the crowd at Fatima at eighteen thousand persons. Many indeed were incredulous, and drawn simply through curiosity; but the majority believed, came to the spot in a spirit of devotion, and during the long time of waiting recited the Rosary and sang hymns. A pious family had built about the tree of the apparitions a rustic arch with two lighted lanterns, and a table with four candles served as an altar.

The disappointment and indignation of this crowd can be imagined when they learned of the kidnapping of the three seers. The most excited were speaking of going over to Ourem and demanding an explanation of the sub-prefect, when in the midst of this agitation certain *mysterious phenomena* occurred which restored calm to their spirits.

At the exact hour of the apparitions the attention of all was drawn to the tree by a loud explosion. Then followed the flash of lightning which usually announced the coming of the Lady. The sun began to lose its brilliance and the atmosphere showed a great array of colours. Meanwhile, a beautiful white cloud appeared above the tree of the apparitions, remained there a moment, and finally rose and disappeared in the air. The crowd was delighted. No one had seen the heavenly Lady, but these extraordinary phenomena, already observed at the previous apparitions, showed clearly that she had come to the meeting-place.

CHAPTER VI

The Fourth Apparition at Valinhos
(August 19th, 1917)

THE little seers did not expect to see the Lady until the thirteenth of the following month. But on Sunday, August 19th, while the impious anticlericals were making their counter-manifestation at Fatima, she appeared to the children as they tended their flock at Valinhos.

She complained first of the wicked man who had prevented them from going to the meeting-place on August 13th, adding that *on that account the miracle promised for October 13th would be less magnificent than was intended.* Then she exhorted them once more to recite the Rosary every day and not to miss the rendezvous on the following months.

She told them that in October they would see St. Joseph with the Child Jesus ready to give peace to the world, that they would see Our Lord blessing the world and that they would also see Our Lady of the Rosary and Our Lady of Dolours.

Lucy asked what should be done with the money which for the first time, on August 13th, had been left at the foot of the tree.

The reply was "Our Lady of the Rosary must be borne in procession and paid great honour."

Continuing to exhort the children to the practice of prayer and penance, the apparition concluded.

"Pray, pray very much, make sacrifices for sinners. Remember that many souls are lost because there is nobody to pray and to make sacrifices for them."

CHAPTER VII

The Fifth Apparition
(*September 13th, 1917*)

THE attack of the Free-thinkers on Fatima had a result quite different from what they had hoped. After the Draconian enquiry by the sub-prefect, and the phenomena observed on August 13th in the children's absence, hardly anyone doubted the sincerity of the little seers and the reality of the apparitions. So on September 13th the crowd was larger than ever in spite of the work in the fields at the harvesting season.

"From the previous evening (September 12th)," writes a witness, "I saw the endless stream of people coming from a distance on foot to Fatima in order to see the apparition on the following day. I was deeply moved, and more than once tears came to my eyes on seeing the piety, the prayers and the ardent faith of the many thousands of pilgrims who recited the Rosary on the way. There was not a road or pathway that was not full of people, and never before in all my life had I witnessed such a glorious and moving manifestation of faith."

On Thursday, September 13th, certain observers estimated the crowd gathered at Fatima at about thirty thousand. The parents of the little seers were present also. All approached the place devoutly and the men uncovered. Almost everybody knelt and prayed fervently.

On her arrival, Lucy said to the crowd:

"You must pray."

"Never shall I forget," writes the same witness, "the deep impression made on me by the sight of all these thousands of pilgrims falling on their knees at the voice of a child of ten, and in tears praying and imploring with confidence the maternal protection of the Queen of Heaven."

At noon, though not a single cloud was to be seen, the glorious sun of this radiant day began to lose its brilliance to such a degree that the *stars were visible!* The atmosphere became a golden yellow. The crowd silently contemplated this wonderful phenomenon which had taken place on the thirteenth of each month since June at the exact moment of the apparitions.

A Globe of Light

The clergy continued to hold themselves prudently aloof from these manifestations. But in face of the growing enthusiasm of the crowds, Mgr. John Quaresma, Vicar General of Leiria, decided to go incognito on this day with another priest to see what took place at Fatima. They remained on the top of the hill, a little apart from the crowd, looking on.

Here is the Vicar General's account:

"The crowd prays all the time . . . Suddenly cries of surprise and joy are heard. Thousands of arms are raised towards a point in the sky.

'Look! There she is.'

'She is here, down there.'

'Do you see?' 'Oh, I see.'

In the sky there is not a single cloud. I raise my eyes and begin to examine the sky closely. My companion says with a tinge of malice:

'There! You are beginning to look, too!'

To my surprise, I see clearly and distinctly, a globe of light advancing from East to West, gliding slowly and majestically through the air. My friend looks also, and he has the good fortune to see the same unexpected vision . . . Suddenly the globe with its wonderful light disappears from my sight, but near us a little girl of ten continues to cry joyfully:

'I still see it, I still see it, now it is going down' (towards the tree of the apparitions).

'What do you think of this globe?' I ask my friend.

'I believe it is the Blessed Virgin', he answers without hesitation . . . This was also my conviction. The children contemplated the Mother of God in person, to us was granted the grace of seeing the vehicle that carried her."

At this moment, a light white cloud was seen to form about the tree, and—*Oh, Miracle!—from the limpid and cloudless sky there began to rain upon those present a shower, as it were, of white flowers, which on coming near the earth vanished without touching it.*

Meanwhile near the tree, Lucy was heard speaking aloud to an invisible being. Some witnesses, who were near enough to the tree, declared that they heard even the whispering of the apparition.

The Heavenly Conversation

The apparition insisted once more on the necessity of continuing the recitation of the Rosary in honour of Our Lady of the Rosary, in order that she might put an end to the war. She renewed her promise to work a great miracle on October 13th in order that all might believe in the apparitions, and asked the children to be there without fail. *Then she repeated that on that day St. Joseph and the infant Jesus would come also to give peace to the world, and that Our Lord would bless the people.*

Some people had asked Lucy to ask the Lady if she would allow part of the alms to be used for building a chapel on the site of the apparitions. The Lady deigned to grant the people's request, and said that one half was to be used for the bier and the other half for the chapel. The child also asked the apparition to cure several sick persons who had been recommended to her.

"I shall heal some of them," she replied, "but not the others because Our Lord does not trust them."

That might mean that the sick persons had not the dispositions of faith, contrition and fervour required for a supernatural cure. It might also mean that for the salvation of certain souls the cross of illness was more useful than healing.

A simple child had asked Lucy to offer the Lady a little bottle of eau-de-Cologne. This she did and the Lady's answer is worth remembering and meditating upon:

"That is not needed in Heaven."

After these words the Lady left and Lucy said to the people: "If you wish to see her, look in that direction."

"Near us," resumes the Vicar General of Leiria, "the same girl cried joyfully: 'She ise going now. She is going up!' And the child continued to point at the luminous globe until it had disappeared in the direction and light of the sun. We felt truly happy. My friend, full of enthusiasm, went from group to group . . . asking the people what they had seen. The persons asked came from the most varied social classes, and all unanimously affirmed the reality of the phenomena which we ourselves had observed."

CHAPTER VIII

The Examination of the Three Seers

THE unpleasant examination by the sub-prefect had established the perfect sincerity of the children. On the other hand, the hypothesis of an illusion on their part could no longer be held since the crowd itself had witnessed the *numerous, varied and wonderful phenomena, which occurred regularly at Fatima at fixed times.* These apparitions at Fatima had become a national event. The homes of the children were literally stormed by visitors—priests, layfolk, lawyers, noble ladies and people of all classes, who wished to see and question them. Among the numerous visitors we single out for special mention the illustrious professor of Theology of the Patriarchal Seminary of Lisbon, Dr. Formigan, commissioned officially by the Patriarchal Curia to follow up closely these events, which were beginning to compel universal attention. He assisted discreetly at the apparition of September 13th, and also at that of October 13th. He went several times to the homes of the three seers, instituting detailed and careful examinations which may be consulted in the works to be indicated shortly. It is sufficient for us to say here that the children's answers were so clear and so frank in their conciseness, so careful in exactness of detail and in such close agreement that it became impossible not to accept their testimony. We give one example:

Dr. Formigan asked Lucy:

"It is said that the Lady already appeared to you last year, is that so?"

"She has never appeared to me, either last year or before the month of May this year, and I have never told that to anyone because it is not true."

"Has she requested that many people be present at the apparitions?"

"No, she has never said anything on that point."

"Francis, do you hear what the Lady says?"

"I only see her; I do not hear anything of what she says."

Similarly one day the Pastor of Porto-de-Moz said to Jacinta:

"Listen, you would not tell us anything, but Lucy has told everything; she has confessed that it is all false."

"No, no" retorted the child, "she did not say that."

"Yes, yes," said the priest, "she has told us everything, it was all made up."

"No, she did not say that," repeated Jacinta, quite sure of herself.

"But she has told us!" insisted the priest.

"No, she did not tell you so," repeated the child with the same assurance.

The Pastor then said to his companion:

"I need no further proofs; this attitude of a child of seven is enough for me."

Bibliography of Fatima

Professor Formigan, who has thus followed the events closely, became the first historian of the events of Fatima.

Among the best historians of Fatima, Rev. Fr. Gonzaga da Fonseca, S.J., professor at the Pontifical Biblical Institute at Rome, himself a Portuguese who knows thoroughly the persons, places and events of which he speaks, wrote in Italian *Le Meraviglie di Fatima*. This book, which is already in its tenth edition, has been translated into Portuguese, English, Spanish, German, etc.

The French edition, translated and adapted by Canon Barthas under the title of *Fatima, Merveille Inouie*, is a history of Fatima, capable of satisfying the just demands of an educated person. We recommend it strongly to the clergy and to the faithful as a work that is gripping as well as useful.

Canon Barthas has also written an admirable life of the three seers of Fatima entitled: *Il était trois petits enfants*. We may add that these two books have received letters of high praise from the Holy See.

All these books, as well as the present booklet, have been translated into several languages. We have really only indicated some of the best books on these enthralling events. The official catalogue of the bibliography on Fatima contains no less than ten pages of small type.

CHAPTER IX

The Great Day
(*October 13th, 1917*)

OCTOBER 13th was to be the decisive day. For it was on this day that the Lady had promised (i) *to say who she was and what she wanted*, (ii) *to work a great miracle that all might believe in her apparitions*. The predictions were now known throughout the country, and all, both believers and scoffers, were thrilled by this bold prediction which promised a great miracle for a definite time and place. It was an easy and effective way of verifying the reality of the apparitions of Fatima. All Portugal awaited, with an understandable curiosity, this conclusive proof of October 13th.

Anticlerical Agitation

In proportion as the popular enthusiasm for the miracles of Fatima grew, the hostility of the Free-thinkers increased. One day three men went to the homes of the children. After an insulting examination they left saying:

"You must make up your minds to tell the secret, for otherwise it has been decided to kill you."

"How good that would be!" cried the intrepid Jacinta. "I love Jesus and the Blessed Virgin Mary so much: we shall go to Them more quickly!"

Other visitors spread more sinister rumours that the children and their parents would be brought before the tribunal for seducing the people; that bombs would be placed near the tree to blow it all up, etc. Frightened by all these threats, Jacinta's parents thought of sending their children away from Fatima, but they refused saying:

"It does not matter if we are killed; we shall go to heaven all the sooner."

On October 11th, Dr. Formigan asked Lucy:

"Do you not fear the anger of the people if the promised miracle is not worked?"

"No," replied the girl frankly, "I have no fear on that score."

On the morrow, October 12th, Lucy's mother, very anxious about these rumours, suggested going to confession so as to be ready for anything.

"If you wish to go to confession," the child answered quietly, "I shall go with you willingly, but I have not the slightest fear. I am sure the Lady will do as she promised."

In face of such calm assurance, the mother spoke no more of confession.

On the morning of October 13th, the big newspaper of Lisbon, "O Seculo," published an ironical article by its director, Avelino d'Almeida, on the apparitions of Fatima, in which he saw only superstition and fraud, while at the same time admitting that the clergy were maintaining a correct attitude, correct "at least in appearance", he added maliciously.

The Crowd of Pilgrims

But none of these measures of intimidation and mockery had any effect on the crowd. From the eve, October 12th, all the roads to Fatima were already packed with carriages, bicycles and an immense crowd of pilgrims reciting the Rosary and singing hymns, on their way to the site of the apparitions, where they were going to spend the night in the open. It might be called a general mobilisation to go and hear the message from heaven, and to see the promised miracle which was to authenticate the message. Though no one knew in what the miracle would consist, each was determined to see it at first hand.

The morning of October 13th was disappointing, for contrary to all expectations, it was wet, gloomy and cold. It seemed as if heaven wished to test the faith and devotion of the pilgrims, and to make them merit, by a hard sacrifice, the honour of witnessing the promised miracle. But the bad weather did not check in any way the crowd that gathered from everywhere, even from the extreme limits of the country; while reporters and photographers from the big newspapers were there to get the facts.

The continuous rain had transformed the place of the apparitions, which is a hollow, into a vast mud-pit; and all, pilgrims or curious, were drenched to the skin or frozen with the cold. Shortly before midday, an observer estimated the crowd at about seventy thousand.

Finally, Lucy said to the people:

"You must close your umbrellas."

They obeyed, and in the pelting rain recited the Rosary.

The Last Apparition

Suddenly, Lucy gives a slight start, and cries:

"There is the lightning."

Then raising her hand she adds:

"See, she is coming! She comes! Do you see her?"

"Look well, my child, take care not to be mistaken," says her mother who, kneeling beside her, is clearly troubled about the issue of this gripping drama; Lucy no longer hears, she is in ecstasy.

Some pious people, with delicate attention, have decorated the tree with flowers and ribbons. In acknowledgment of this act of loving homage the Lady places her feet on these ornaments. Meanwhile, the rain has ceased, and the crowd can see a light white cloud, which, like the smoke of incense, forms round the little seers, rises to a height of about fifteen feet, and scatters in the air. This phenomenon occurs three times, as if an invisible priest was there incensing the heavenly apparition liturgically.

Lucy then asks the question the Lady had promised to answer on that day:

"Madam, who are you and what do you want of me"?

The Message

Then the Lady answers:

"I am Our Lady of the Rosary; I want a chapel built here in my honour. Continue to say the Rosary every day."

She adds that the war is coming to an end and that the soldiers will not be long in returning to their homes.

Preoccupied by all the commissions given her by the people, Lucy interrupts:

"I have so many favours to ask you."

The Blessed Virgin answers that she will grant some, but not all, and immediately continues the message:

"Men must amend their lives, and ask pardon for their sins."

Then, with a look of grief, and in a suppliant tone of voice:

"Men must not offend God any more for He is already very much offended."

The Multiple Vision

Then taking leave of the little seers, the Blessed Virgin opens her hands, which throw beams of light towards the sun. At the moment of the commencement of the solar prodigy, of which we shall speak shortly, the children see another apparition which unfolds itself beside the sun in three successive scenes.

They see first the three members of the *Holy Family,* in this order: to the right of the sun and more brilliant than it Our Lady of the Rosary in a white dress and a blue mantle, and at the left dressed in red is St. Joseph with the Infant Jesus blessing the world. Then Lucy sees at the right of the sun Our Divine Lord as a full-grown man, lovingly blessing the world, and at the left *Our Lady of the Seven Dolours.* Finally Our Lady of the Seven Dolours is replaced by *Our Lady of Mount Carmel,* the scapular in her hand.

It has been asked why the Blessed Virgin, who appeared always under the same aspect, had wished on this occasion to appear first with the Holy Family, then as Our Lady of the Seven Dolours, finally as Our Lady of Mount Carmel. The usual answer, as we shall see later, is that Our Lady wished, in this manner, to impress more deeply on the minds of the faithful the title of Our Lady of the Rosary, which she gave herself at Fatima, recalling in the three successive scenes the three sets of mysteries, joyful, sorrowful and glorious, on which we meditate when we recite the Rosary.

CHAPTER X

The Great Solar Prodigy

"The Sun Dances"

At the end of the apparition, "the Blessed Virgin opened her hands which threw beams of light on the sun." Instinctively Lucy cried:

"Oh! look at the sun!"

No one was thinking of the sun, which had not appeared all the morning. But at the child's exclamation, all raised their heads to see what was taking place. Then this vast multitude was able to contemplate at leisure for about twelve minutes, a grand spectacle, stupendous and truly unique.

Immediately the clouds opened wide, exposing an immense surface of blue. In the cloudless area the sun appeared at its zenith, but with a strange aspect. For though not a single cloud veiled it, yet while being very bright, it was not dazzling, and you could look straight at it at will. Everybody looked in surprise at this new kind of eclipse.

Suddenly the sun trembles, is shaken, makes some abrupt movements, and finally begins to turn giddily on itself like a wheel of fire, casting in all directions, like an enormous lamp, great beams of light. These beams are in turn green, red, blue, violet, etc., and colour in a most fantastic manner the clouds, trees, rocks, the earth, the clothes and faces of this immense crowd, which extends as far as the eye can see. And while the breathless crowd contemplates this amazing spectacle, the children see beside the sun three scenes already described.

After about four minutes the sun stops. A moment later it resumes *a second time* its fantastic motion, and its fairy-like dance of light and colour such as could never be imagined in the most gorgeous display of fireworks. Once more, after a few minutes, the sun stops its prodigious dance, as if to give the spectators a rest.

After a short stop and for the *third time*, as if to give them an opportunity of examining the facts carefully, the sun takes up again, more varied and colourful than ever, its fantastic display of fireworks, without a doubt the most glorious and most moving that has ever been seen on this earth.

All through these unforgettable twelve minutes, during which this unique and gripping spectacle lasts, the enormous multitude is there in suspense, immovable, almost in ecstasy, breathless, contemplating this moving drama, which was seen distinctly within a radius of more than twenty-five miles.

This was the great miracle promised, which took place precisely at the time and place fixed, and which was to compel men to believe in the reality of the apparitions, and to obey the message which Our Lady of the Rosary brought them from heaven.

The Fall of the Sun

The sight of this wonderful miracle had already well disposed all hearts and excited in them the most noble religious sentiments of lively faith in the power of God, of sincere adoration of His infinite majesty, and of absolute trust in the message of Fatima, so majestically confirmed. But all this was, as it were, a preparation for the total renewal of souls.

It was the terrible fall of the sun which was the culminating point of the great miracle, the most awful moment, and the most divinely moving, which finally brought many souls completely back to God by a sincere act of contrition and love.

Indeed in the midst of its crazy dance of fire and colours, like a gigantic wheel which from spinning has swung off its axis, so now the *sun leaves its place in the firmament, and falling from side to side, plunges zigzagging upon the crowd below,* sending out a heat increasingly intense, and giving to the spectators a clear impression of the scene at the end of the world foretold in the Gospel, when the sun and the stars will fall in disorder upon the earth.

Then from this terrified crowd there suddenly escapes a terrible cry, an immense shout, betraying the religious terror of souls preparing seriously for death, confessing their faith and asking God pardon for their sins.

"I believe in God the Father Almighty," cry some.

"Hail Mary!" cry others.

"My God, mercy!" implore a large number.

Many of the people falling on their knees in the mud, recite in a voice choking with sobs the most sincere act of contrition that has ever come from their hearts.

Finally, stopping short in its vertiginous fall, the sun climbs back to its place, zigzagging as it had come down, and ends by gradually regaining its usual brilliance set in a limpid sky.

Moving detail: this apocalyptic scene full of majesty and terror, ended with a delicate gift, which shows the motherly tenderness of the Heart of Mary for her children. Though all had been drenched to the skin, each now had the pleasant surprise of feeling quite comfortable, his clothes being *absolutely dry*.[1]

It is reported in Holy Scripture that when Moses came down from Sinai, his face was still quite radiant with traces of the Divine colloquy. At Fatima also this vast multitude that had just witnessed wonders worthy of Sinai, departed gradually, happy, restrained, recollected, all radiant still from the Divine contact which had just renewed their souls in a new baptism of faith, confidence, contrition and love, whose fiery impressions will remain forever ineffaceable.

[1] This wonderful fact already authenticated in the official canonical process is also confirmed by Marquis da Cruz, member of the Academy, who made a personal investigation of this point.

CHAPTER XI

Other Accounts of the Great Prodigy

1. His Lordship the Bishop of Leiria

IN his pastoral letter of October 13th, 1930, approving the apparitions and the cult of Our Lady of Fatima, His Lordship the Bishop of Leiria, after various considerations, comes to the great solar prodigy which he summarises in these terms:

"The solar phenomenon on October 13th, 1917, described in the newspapers of the period, was the most wonderful of all and was the one that made the profoundest impression on all those who had the privilege of witnessing it. The three children had foretold the place and time at which it was to occur, and their prediction had soon spread throughout the whole of Portugal, so that, though the day was gloomy and wet, thousands and thousands of persons betook themselves to Fatima at the hour of the last apparition. And this crowd witnessed all the manifestations of the royal star, which thus paid homage to the Queen of Heaven and Earth, more bright than the sun at the height of its brilliance, as we read in the Canticle of Canticles. This phenomenon, which was not registered by any observatory, and was therefore not of the natural order, persons of all conditions and of all social classes saw with their own eyes . . . even persons who were several miles away, a fact which precludes any explanation by means of a collective illusion."

2. A Missionary

In his book, *Our Lady of Fatima*, Fr. Fonseca, S.J., quotes extracts from a letter of Fr. Ignatius Lawrence Pereira, a missionary in the Indies, dated July 13th, 1931:

"These events took place fourteen years ago, yet I still retain very clearly in my memory the profound impressions produced on my youthful mind by the wonderful solar spectacle of October 13th, 1917. I was hardly nine years of age, and went to the primary school in my village perched on a

46

lonely hill just opposite Fatima, about six or seven miles away . . . towards midday we were alarmed by the cries and shouts of the passers-by . . . Our teacher rushed out, and the children all ran after her. In the public square people wept and shouted pointing to the sun, without paying the slightest heed to the questions of our teacher . . . It was the great solar prodigy with all its wonderful phenomena which was seen distinctly even from the hill on which my village was situated. This miracle I feel incapable of describing such as I saw it at that moment. I looked fixedly at the sun, which appeared pale and did not dazzle. It looked like a ball of snow turning on itself. . . Then suddenly it seemed to become detached from the sky, and rolled right and left, as if it were falling upon the earth. Terrified, absolutely terrified, I ran towards the crowd of people. All were weeping, expecting at any moment the end of the world.

"Quite near to us was an unbeliever, who had just spent the morning jeering at those he saw going to Fatima. I watched him. He stood there as if paralysed, stunned, staring at the sun. I then saw him shiver from head to foot, raise his hands to heaven, and fall on his knees in the mud crying:

'Holy Virgin, Holy Virgin.'

"Meanwhile, the people continued to weep and cry, asking God pardon for their sins. Then they turned their steps in the direction of the two little chapels of the village which in a few moments were quite full. During the long minutes of the solar phenomenon, the objects around us reflected all the colours of the rainbow. Looking at each other, one appeared blue, another yellow, a third red, etc., and all these strange phenomena only increased the terror of the people. After about ten minutes the sun climbed back into its place, as it had descended, still quite pale and without brilliance.

"When the people were convinced that the danger had passed, there was an outburst of joy. All shouted:

'A miracle! A miracle! Praised be the Blessed Virgin!' "

3. The Newspaper: *O Seculo*

". . . Then we witness a spectacle unique and incredible for one who was not present. . . The sun resembles a dull silver plate. . . It does not warm, it does not dazzle. One

47

would say that an eclipse had occurred. But now a loud shout is heard:

'Miracle, Miracle!'

"Before the astonished eyes of this crowd, whose attitude takes us back to Biblical times, and who, pale with fear and with heads bare, look at the azure sky, the sun trembles, the sun makes abrupt movements, never seen before, and outside all cosmic laws, the sun 'begins to dance' as the peasants say. . . Only one thing remains now to be done, namely, for the scientists to explain from the height of their learning the fantastic dance of the sun, which, to-day at Fatima, has drawn 'Hosanna' from the hearts of the faithful; and which, as trustworthy people assure me, has impressed even Free-thinkers, as well as others of no religious convictions, who had come to this spot, henceforth celebrated." (Avelino d'Almeida).[1]

4. The Newspaper: *O Dia*

"The clouds were rent and the sun like a silver disc began to revolve on itself and zigzag in a circle of the sky free from clouds. A great cry arose from the hearts of all present and the thousands of people, of a most lively faith, fell on their knees on the wet ground. The light of the sun became a strange blue; one would have said that it came through the stained-glass windows of an immense cathedral, before diffusing itself in this gigantic nave shaped as an arch by all the hands raised heavenwards. Then the blue light gradually shaded to appear as if filtered through yellow stained-glass windows. Some yellow specks now fell on the white headdresses and on the dark tresses of the women. These specks multiplied themselves indefinitely on trees, stones, on the sun. . . The whole crowd wept, the whole crowd prayed, the men with their caps in hand, in the glorious accomplishment of the expected miracle."

[1] Avelino d'Almeida, director of "O Seculo," has written that very morning in this newspaper the ironical article mentioned earlier. At noon he witnessed the solar prodigy, at Cova da Iria, and that evening, while still under the influence of the morning's events, wrote the new article from which we have quoted some extracts. This article published in "O Seculo" of Monday, October 15th, created a sensation throughout the country, and drew on its author sharp reproaches from Free-thinkers, who did not pardon him for giving such publicity to the events of Fatima, and for supporting them with his authority.

5. Marquis da Cruz

In his book, the *Virgin of Fatima,* this illustrious author reports several authoritative witnesses.

He quotes first his own sister:

"On October 13th, 1917, I arrived at Fatima. It had rained all the morning, but in spite of the bad weather there was a crowd. Near me a priest looked at his watch, saying:

" 'Poor children! They have been mistaken: the time fixed is passing; there is no miracle.'

"But lo! the rain suddenly ceased, and the sun came out throwing its rays on the earth. It seemed to fall on the heads of this multitude, and turned on itself like a wheel of fire in a fireworks display. Our faces, our clothes, and even the earth itself, everything assumed the same fantastic colour. The people wept and cried. This unique spectacle lasted about a quarter of an hour. Deeply moved I myself cried out:

" 'O my God how great is Your power!'

"And at the same instant I saw *St. Joseph* with the Infant Jesus in his arms, in the centre of the sun, which, ceasing to turn, resumed its natural colour, but could still be looked at like the moon without the slightest inconvenience. I was not the only one to see these prodigies; the whole crowd saw them. Everything then had occurred as the little seers had foretold. After this miracle, I saw on May 13th, 1918, white balls descending from heaven. On another May 13th, *I also saw many rose-petals falling.* They came from the sun in large quantities. When high in the air they were large, but on approaching us they became small and vanished. Men held out their hats to collect them, but when they tried to hold them they found nothing. One of these petals fell on my left shoulder. I tried to take it quickly in my hand, but found nothing."

Marquis da Cruz also quotes this evidence:

"The brilliant poet Alfonso Lopes Vieira related to us on the evening of October 30th, 1935, on the balcony of his beautiful house of Sao Pedro der Muel, which is thirty miles from Fatima:

" 'On this day, October 13th, 1917, I had forgotten the prediction of the three shepherds, when I was surprised and charmed by a spectacle in the sky, truly astounding, for me entirely unheard of, which I witnessed from this balcony.' "

The Marquis da Cruz continues:

"This enormous multitude was drenched, for it had rained unceasingly since dawn. But—though this may appear incredible—after the great miracle everyone felt comfortable, and found his garments quite dry, a subject of general wonder. . . The truth of this fact has been guaranteed with the greatest sincerity by dozens and dozens of persons of absolute trustworthiness, whom I have known intimately from childhood, and who are still alive (1937), as well as by persons from various districts of the country who were present."

6. The Testimony of the Learned

Dr. Almeida Garrete, Professor at the University of Coimbra, writes:

"I was at a distance of little more than a hundred yards away. The rain was pouring down on our heads and, streaming down our clothes, soaked them completely. At last it came along to 2 o'clock, p.m. (official time—really corresponding to noon, solar time). Some instants previously, the radiant sun had pierced the thick curtain of clouds which held it veiled. All eyes were raised towards it as if drawn by a magnet. I myself tried to look straight at it, and saw it looking like a well-defined disc, bright but not blinding. I heard people around me comparing it to a dull silver plate. The comparison did not seem to me exact. Its appearance was of a sharp and changing clarity, like the 'Orient' of a pearl. It did not resemble in any way the moon on a fine night. It had neither its colour nor its shadows. You might compare it rather to a polished wheel cut in the silvery valves of a shell. This is not poetry, I saw it thus with my own eyes.

"Neither would you confuse it with the sun seen through a for. Of fog there was no trace, and besides, the solar disc was neither blurred nor veiled in any way, but shone clearly at its centre and at its circumference.

"This chequered shining disc seemed to possess a giddy motion. It was not the twinkling of a star. It turned on itself with an astonishing rapidity.

"Suddenly a great cry, like a cry of anguish, arose from all this vast throng. The sun while keeping its swiftness of rotation, detached itself from the firmament and, blood-red in colour, rushed towards the earth, threatening to crush us under the immense weight of its mass of fire. These were moments of dreadful tension.

"All these phenomena, which I have described, I have witnessed personally, coldly and calmly, without the slightest agitation of mind."

The writer Leopold Nunes points out that:

"Here and there, at Cova da Iria, under the trees, near the road, or sheltered from the rain in their motor-cars, were members of the highest level of the literary, artistic and scientific world, mostly unbelievers, who had come through curiosity, drawn by the prediction of the three little seers."

This testimony is confirmed by Marquis da Cruz who adds:

"Several learned people who had witnessed this spectacle frankly admitted: 'I have seen, but I cannot explain it.'"

This admission is worth remembering. It proves, in fact, that the events of Fatima, and in particular the precise announcement of the great miracle for noon on October 13th, had caused such a sensation in the country that even learned people could not resist their curiosity to go and examine the facts on the spot. And these representatives of learning who testify to having seen and verified the undeniable reality of the prodigies, frankly admit that these facts of Fatima are beyond them!

This admission comes from people of the weightiest authority. Yet is it not annoying to hear learned men declare, even after the events, entire ignorance of their cause, while three little shepherds of seven, nine and ten years knew several months previously, and announced with absolute certainty that "at noon on October 13th a great miracle would take place at Cova da Iria, in order that all might believe in the apparitions"?

The Necessary Conclusions

For an honest mind, it is not difficult to find the cause of these wonderful prodigies. It is Our Lady of the Rosary of Fatima who announced them to the three little shepherds in a precise manner; it is she therefore who at a given moment performed them. Such is the wonderful miracle of Fatima which has been called the "greatest event of the century."

Indeed, it could be called the most wonderful event in the history of the Church after the sublime scenes of Calvary, the Ascension and Pentecost. Nothing need be added to such prodigies. All human comment could only lessen its wonder.

We shall see later that the wonderful apparitions of Fatima have been confirmed by ecclesiastical approbation after a minute canonical investigation, and an official examination of the facts which lasted until October, 1930.

It now remains for us to explain the meaning of the Prodigy and of the heavenly Message of Fatima. We shall then indicate in a third part how the events have given rise to the great pilgrimages which each year lead one Portuguese out of every six to the sanctuary of Our Lady of the Rosary of Fatima.

PART II

THE MESSAGE

CHAPTER I

The Meaning of the Great Prodigy

The Sign in the Heavens

THE Holy Gospel relates that the Pharisees, wishing to fix conditions for Our Lord's miracles, one day demanded that He cause before them a sign in the sky. In His merciful goodness Our Divine Lord deigned to offer them the great sign of His Resurrection, while refusing to submit to the proud demands of the creature who dared to lay down conditions for his Creator. This wonderful sign in the heavens, which was refused to the insolent Pharisees, Our Lady of the Rosary of Fatima has maternally granted to the modern world "in order that all may believe."

The apparitions and miracles of the Blessed Virgin are frequent and well known in history. The list of the principal ones that have taken place since the beginning of the last century is impressive: 1830 the Miraculous Medal; 1836 Our Lady of Victories; 1846 La Salette; 1858 Lourdes; 1871 Pontmain; 1876 Pellevoisin; 1917 Fatima. *But what is truly unique in Fatima is the stupendous character of this sign in the heavens.* In the presence of such a prodigy we wonder instinctively what great religious crisis is facing the world: for surely it is some such crisis in our own times which caused the Mother of God to intervene, manifesting the Almighty Power of God in a manner so wonderful that those who witnessed it really believed that they were seeing the end of the world.

After reading the "Angel's Prayer" and certain passages of the Secret of Fatima which we shall see shortly, the reader will have no difficulty in discovering the great danger of the present day against which Heaven warned us in 1917. Clearly indicated in this foreshadowing of the future we see all these modern currents of the Atheist, Bolshevist, Communist and other anti-Christian movements, whose programme is "not to believe, nor adore, nor hope, nor love." It is they who, with impious hate, shake their fists against heaven, making it their aim to destroy by all means in their power the Catholic Faith, as well as the Catholic Church and the Catholic Priesthood, whose mission is precisely to preach this faith to all nations even to the end of time.

"Note the coincidence," writes Fr. Fonseca. "On April 16th, 1917, Lenin and Trotsky arrived in Petrograd, and on the following days they gave its orientation to the communist revolution which they directed. On November 7th, the same year, the Bolshevist faction triumphed first at Petrograd, then at Moscow, and in its fight against God, purposed to drench in blood and fire, Russia, Mexico, the Iberian Peninsula (Spain and Portugal) . . . then the entire world.

"It is between these two dates—exactly twenty-seven days after the first, and twenty-five days before the second—that the first and last apparitions took place at Fatima.

"This means that: when in the eastern end of Europe anti-Christ unloosed, not only against the true religion, but even against the very idea of God and against civil society, the most terrible onslaught in all history, *at that same moment there appeared in splendour at the western extremity, the Great and Eternal Enemy of the infernal serpent!*"

She came solemnly to remind us of the unique and infallible means of salvation, strengthening our faith in God, inviting us to prayer and penance and to flee sin, asking us to recite the Rosary daily and to consecrate ourselves to her Immaculate Heart.

Fatima Should Revive Our Faith

By the exceptional grandeur of the prodigy of Fatima, the Blessed Virgin would revive our fainting faith, and make it invincible against the seduction of all these modern anti-Christian movements, which, disguised under various names, seek to set up on earth a new conception of the world, a new order, a new morality, a new religion, which is really a total denial of God and all religion. The grandeur of this wonderful prodigy of Fatima will thus be in proportion to the greatness of the dangers that threaten the world, and *this sign in the heavens* will indicate to us the remedy we are to employ against the evils that hang over us.

Already, on October 13th, 1917, Avelino d'Almeida observed in his article in *O Seculo,* that the direct and immediate effect of the great solar prodigy had been to revive in an extraordinary manner the faith of the faithful, and to make unbelievers reflect seriously. Here are some passages from his article: "Beside me a venerable old man, whose gentle and majestic features recalled Paul Déroulède, contemplated the sun. He began to recite the 'I believe in God', which he continued in a loud voice to the end. Then addressing some neighbours who still kept their hats on, he begged them 'vehemently' *to uncover before such an extraordinary demonstration of the existence of God!"* And after saying that similar scenes had taken place at other parts of Cova da Iria, the same journalist continued: "The sign in the heavens has been enough to satisfy those present, and to confirm them in their 'Breton peasant's faith'. . . And returning to their homes they went, 'their souls full of adoration,' to carry the good news to the villages that had not been entirely emptied of their inhabitants. . ."

In imitation of those happy pilgrims of Fatima, let us in turn respectfully bow down before this prodigy of the sign in the heavens, before this "extraordinary demonstration of the existence of God." *Let us meditate long on these divine facts: let us enkindle the flame of our faith in the mysterious rays of the Sun of Fatima.* Let us also return from this holy pilgrimage, our souls full of adoration, penetrated through and through by the Sovereign transcendence of God, Who makes even the sun to tremble. Full of sentiments of profound respect, let us offer to God the conscious homage of our "Credo". Let us adore Him by the perfect docility of our minds to the truths of revelation; by the entire submission of our wills to the divine precepts; by the absolute dependence of our whole being on His Sovereign Majesty. Like the happy witnesses of the prodigy of Fatima, let us be proud to confess our holy Faith, to show ourselves in our lives openly Christian; to proclaim ourselves the faithful adorers of God and of His Son Jesus Christ, our sole Master and Lord. And if amidst all these anti-Christian movements, we receive one day, like the martyrs, the inestimable grace of being able to give to our Divine Master the supreme testimony of our lives, let us then consider ourselves happy! As we shall have confessed Him before men, He will confess us before His Father Who is in heaven! Heaven and earth will pass away, but His words will not pass away.

CHAPTER II

Official Publication on the Mystery of Fatima

FOR a long time relatively little was known of the mystery of Fatima—a few circumstances of the apparitions, the external prodigies, the words of the message of October 13th, 1917. The little seers had always kept carefully hidden, not only the secret confided to them by the apparition, but also many details edifying as well as instructive.

Francis died in 1919 of the well-known Spanish influenza, followed shortly by Jacinta; and last of all Lucy retired to a convent. All hope then seemed to be lost of ever arriving at a knowledge not only of the secret but also of the most intimate details of the heavenly colloquies of Fatima.

But what the humility of the seers sought to keep hidden, Divine Providence has revealed for the greater good of souls.

First Revelations

On December 17th, 1927, Lucy asked Our Lord in the Blessed Sacrament how she could obey her spiritual director, who had asked her to set down in writing certain graces of God, when among them was the secret confided to her by Our Lady of Fatima. Jesus caused her to hear clearly an interior voice saying: "Write, My child, what is asked of you. Write also all that the Blessed Virgin has revealed to you about the devotion to the Immaculate Heart of Mary. As for the rest of the secret, continue for the moment to keep that hidden."

Later, at the request of His Lordship the Bishop of Leiria-Fatima, Lucy wrote also her souvenirs of Jacinta and Francis.

Lastly, on the approach of the twenty-fifth anniversary of the apparitions, His Lordship once more requested Lucy to write an exact account of the apparitions, "without omitting anything that can now be revealed."

Lucy's Revelations

Sending to His Lordship the documents requested Lucy wrote on December 8th, 1941: "I believe, my Lord, that I have related all that your Excellency has ordered me to write for the present. So far I have always done my best to hide the most intimate facts in the apparitions of Fatima. Each time that I was obliged to speak about them, I tried to touch on them only lightly so as not to reveal what I desired so much to keep hidden. But now that obedience obliges me, here it is. May Almighty God and the Immaculate Heart of Mary deign to accept these poor sacrifices, which They have condescended to ask of me, to re-awaken in souls the spirit of Faith, of Confidence, and of Love."

At the beginning of 1942, on the occasion of the Jubilee celebrations of the apparitions of Fatima, the competent ecclesiastical authority judged it useful for the good of souls to have published a good summary of these different writings of Lucy. That is why, in the fourth edition of his book, *Le Meraviglie di Fatima,* published April 13th, 1942, Fr. Fonseca, S.J., has been able to reveal to us a number of facts of the highest interest, throwing great light on the Mystery of Fatima. One could not help being moved on reading these new accounts of the apparitions of the angel, of the heroic virtues of the little ones, and of the famous "secret" of which only a last portion now remains hidden—for the present.

In the following chapters which give these last revelations, we hardly do more than translate the work, so highly authorised, of Fr. Fonseca. But we shall make use of the sixth edition which gives the last details made public by His Lordship the Bishop of Leiria-Fatima.

CHAPTER III

Preparation by the Angel

THE latest documents reveal to us that for quite a long time before the great apparitions of the Blessed Virgin at Fatima, the three children had begun to receive the unexpected visit of an angel who prepared them for their future mission.

The first world war had already lasted two years when, at the beginning of March, 1916, a refugee ship interned in the Portuguese island of Madeira made its escape. In order to prevent further evasions, Portugal seized all the ships that had sought refuge in her ports. On March 9th, the Central Powers declared war on her.

The Angel of Peace

Shortly after this, towards "the end of Spring, 1916", while Portugal prepared itself feverishly for war, the three future seers of Fatima were tending their sheep one day on the slopes of the hill of Cabeco. Towards midday, during a shower, they took shelter in a cave in the trees. After dining and reciting the Rosary, they came out once more to go and play.

A violent gust of wind made them raise their heads, and they saw take shape in the air and come towards them a beautiful white cloud in human form, resembling a statue of snow, which the sun made transparent like crystal. As the apparition approached, the children saw a young man of fourteen to sixteen years of age, and of a superhuman beauty.

"Fear not," said he to them, *"I am the Angel of Peace.* Pray with me." Then kneeling and placing his forehead on the ground he said three times: "My God, I believe, I adore, I trust, I love you! I ask pardon for those who do not believe, nor adore, nor trust, nor love You."

Then rising he said: "Pray thus. The holy Hearts of Jesus and Mary will allow themselves to be touched by your supplications."

"The Angel departed," adds Lucy, "but his words remained so deeply imprinted in our minds that we were never able to

59

forget them. From this day onward we often remained prostrate for long hours in the Angel's attitude repeating this prayer, until sometimes we fell exhausted."

Second Apparition of the Angel

On another occasion, in the month of July or August, 1916, the three children were playing together near the well in Lucy's garden, when the same Angel suddenly appeared and said to them: "What are you doing? Pray, pray very much: the holy Hearts of Jesus and Mary have designs of mercy on you! Offer continually to the Lord prayers and sacrifices in reparation for the numerous sins which offend Him, and in supplication for the conversion of sinners. Try then to bring peace to your country. *I am its Guardian Angel. Above all accept and bear with submission the sufferings which it will please the Lord to send you.*"

"Those words," writes Lucy, "engraved themselves on our minds like a living light, making us understand: *how much the good God loves us, how much He wishes to be loved by us, how great is the value of sacrifices, and how by them the Lord converts sinners.*

"Henceforth we made a habit of offering to the Lord whatever mortified us . . . and we continued to repeat each day the Angel's prayer for long hours. . ."

Third Apparition of the Angel

Two or three months later the children had once more led their sheep to the hill of Cabeco. After dinner they retired to the cave to say the Rosary and spend a part of the afternoon reciting the Angel's prayer.

They had already recited this prayer several times, when they were suddenly surrounded by an extraordinary light. Rising they saw the Angel, who held in his hands a chalice, surmounted by a Host, from which drops of Blood fell into the chalice . . . Leaving the chalice and Host suspended in mid-air, the Angel knelt beside the children and made them recite three times the following prayer: "Most Holy Trinity, Father, Son and Holy Spirit, I adore You profoundly! I offer You the most Precious Body and Blood, Soul and Divinity of Our Lord

Jesus Christ, present in all the tabernacles of the world, in reparation for all the outrages committed against It; and by the infinite merits of His Sacred Heart, through the intercession of the Immaculate Heart of Mary, I pray for the conversion of poor sinners!"

Then, rising, he took the Host which he gave to Lucy, and the chalice which he divided between Jacinta and Francis, saying: "Receive the Body and Blood of Jesus Christ horribly outraged by ungrateful men. Make reparation for their sins and console your God."

Prostrating himself once more as if in thanksgiving, the Angel said again three times the prayer, "Most Holy Trinity, Father, Son and Holy Spirit, etc. . ."

Francis, who did not hear the Angel, asked Lucy: "The Angel gave you Holy Communion but what did he give Jacinta and me?" Jacinta, full of joy, answered: "But it is the same thing, Holy Communion! Did you not see that it was the Blood which fell from the Host?" Then Francis, as if communing with himself: "I felt that God was in me, but I did not know in what way."

The children remained prostrate in adoration, not ceasing to repeat the prayers of the first and last apparitions, which they united in one.

Intimately seized by a deep supernatural recollection, they remained, thus absorbed in prayer, and strangers to the exterior world . . . And during these long hours of prayer in the cave, their thirty sheep tended themselves all alone in a mysterious fashion.

At last, Francis, seeing that night was approaching, invited his companions to return home with the flock.

What is the meaning of these extraordinary visits of the Angel, whose reality is guaranteed for us by the authentic documents published at Fatima and at Rome? "It is evident," says Fr. Fonseca, "that they were but a preparation and an orientation. *They prepared for the great apparitions* of Our Lady of Fatima in 1917, and they *directed the prayer* of the three children against the future assaults of the great modern pagan movements, which profess "not to believe, nor adore, nor trust, nor love."

CHAPTER IV

The Secret of Fatima

The First Secret

SINCE the second apparition, on June 13th, 1917, the three children were heard to speak of a "secret". We know now that it was only a "first secret".

Lucy had besought the Lady to take them all with her to heaven. "Yes", she replied, "I shall come soon to take Jacinta and Francis. But you must remain longer on earth. Jesus wishes to use you in making me known and loved. *He wishes to spread in the world devotion to my Immaculate Heart*".

"Then I must remain here below all alone?" the child asked sadly.

"No, my child . . . I shall never abandon you. My Immaculate Heart will be your refuge and the way that will lead you to God."

Lucy adds that in saying these words the *Blessed Virgin opened her hands* as on May 13th, and for the second time projected on the children that immense light in which they saw themselves as if immersed in God. Francis and Jacinta seemed to be in the beam which went up to heaven, and Lucy in the light which spread itself over the earth. In front of the right hand of the apparition was seen a *Heart surrounded with thorns*, which pierced it on all sides. The children understood that it was the Immaculate Heart of Mary, afflicted by the numberless sins of the world, and that it demanded penance and reparation. "On June 13th," observes Lucy, "the Blessed Virgin did not explicitly tell us to keep these things secret, but we felt that Our Divine Lord was urging us to be silent about them."

The Second and Principal Secret

It was on July 13th, 1917, at the third apparition, that the Blessed Virgin confided to the children a real secret, forbidding them to tell anyone.

According to Fr. Fonseca's sixth edition, this is what Lucy writes "in pure obedience and with the permission of heaven":

"The secret consists of three distinct parts", intimately connected. "I shall reveal the first two parts", that is, the vision of hell and devotion to the Immaculate Heart of Mary. The third must remain secret for the present.

(a) The Vision of Hell

"The Blessed Virgin opened her hands once more as on the preceding months, saying the words, 'Sacrifice yourselves for sinners and say often, especially when you make sacrifices: O Jesus, it is for love of You, for the conversion of sinners and in reparation for the offences committed against the Immaculate Heart of Mary.'

"The beam of light projected seemed to penetrate the earth, and we saw as it were a vast sea of fire, in which were, plunged, all blackened and burnt, demons and souls in human form like transparent brands. Raised into the air by the flames they fell back in all directions, like sparks in a huge fire, without weight or poise, amidst loud cries and horrible groans of pain and despair which caused us to shudder and tremble with fear. (It is probably at this scene that I cried, 'Oh!' which those present say they heard). The demons were distinguished by the horrible and repellent forms of terrible unknown animals, like brands of fire black yet transparent.

"This scene lasted an instant, and we must thank Our Heavenly Mother who had prepared us beforehand by promising to take us to heaven with her; otherwise I believe that we should have died of fear and terror."

(b) Devotion to the Immaculate Heart of Mary

"As if looking for help," continues Lucy, "we raised our suppliant eyes towards the Blessed Virgin, who told us kindly but very sadly:

" 'You have just seen hell where the souls of sinners go. To save them the Lord wishes to establish in the world the devotion to my Immaculate Heart. If people do what I shall tell you, many souls will be saved and there will be peace.

" 'The war (of 1914) will soon end. But if men do not stop

63

offending the Lord, it will not be long before another and worse one, begins:[1] that will be in the reign of Pius XI.'

" 'When you see the night illuminated by an unknown light[2] know that it is the great sign which God is giving you, indicating that the world, on account of its innumerable crimes, will soon be punished by war, famine, and persecutions against the Church and the Holy Father.

" 'In order to stop it, I shall come to ask for the consecration of Russia to my Immaculate Heart, as well as Communion of reparation on the first Saturdays of the month.

"If my wishes are fulfilled", the Lady continued, "Russia will be converted and there will be peace; if not, then Russia will spread her errors throughout the world, bringing new wars and persecution of the Church; the good will be martyred and the Holy Father will have much to suffer; certain nations will be annihilated. *But in the end my Immaculate Heart will triumph.* The Holy Father will consecrate Russia to me, and she will be converted, and the world will enjoy a period of peace. In Portugal the faith will always be preserved. Remember, you must not tell this to anyone except Francisco."

After a few moments she added: "When you recite the Rosary *say at the end of each decade:*

"O my Jesus, forgive us our sins, save us from the fire of hell, lead all souls to heaven, and help especially those who most need Your mercy."

Lucy Throws Light on Certain Points

In 1924 the Canonical Commission of Inquiry pointedly asked Lucy if she was quite sure that the Blessed Virgin herself really appeared. Lucy replied with assurance:

"I am certain that I have seen her and that I am making no mistake. Even if I were to be killed no one would make me say otherwise."

[1] It will be remembered that Francis saw the Apparition but did not hear it.

[2] It was in the Pontificate of Pius XI that the terrible Spanish war took place, which was a prelude to the actual world war. Excluding the soldiers who died on the field of battle, the Spanish Reds massacred cruelly thirteen prelates, seven thousand priests or religious, and hundreds of thousands of good Christians, martyrs for their faith.

64

In 1946 several historians of Fatima were able to secure more precise information on certain important points from Sister Lucy, such as the following:

Q. "When did you receive from heaven permission to disclose the secret?"

A. "In 1927, here at Tuy, in the chapel; but the permission did not apply to the third part of the secret."

Q. "Have you spoken of it, then, to your Father Confessor?"

A. "Yes—at once."

Q. "What did he say?"

A. "He commanded me to write the secret—except the third part. I think he did not read it. He gave it back to me. Shortly after I had another Spiritual Director who ordered me to burn it; after which he ordered me to write it again!"

Sister Lucy smiled while recalling these episodes.

Q. "It seems regrettable that the secret was not published before the war?"

A. Lucy replied: "That would have appeared regrettable indeed if the Good God had wanted to present me to the world as a prophetess; but I believe that was not His intention. Moreover, I think that in 1917 He could have commanded me to speak, whereas He commanded me to keep silent, and His order has been confirmed by His representatives. I think then . . . that God did not want to make use of me except to remind the world of avoiding sin and of making reparation for offences against God by prayer and penance. Besides . . . I would, perhaps, have spoiled God's work. Silence has been for me a great grace. I thank the Good God for it; and I find that everything He does is well done!"

Q. "When writing the secret, have you quoted literally the words of the Blessed Virgin?"

A. "Yes; when I write, I try to quote literally. I have then wished to write the secret, word for word".

Q. "Are you sure of having recounted all of it?"

A. "I think so, and I have written the words in the same order as that in which they were said."

Q. "Did the Blessed Virgin really mention the name of Pius XI?"

A. "Yes. We did not then know if he were a pope or a king; but the Blessed Virgin spoke of Pius XI."

Q. "But the war did not begin during the reign of Pius XI?"

A. "The annexation of Austria was the decisive cause.

When the Treaty of Munich was concluded, my sisters (religious) rejoiced saying that peace had been preserved. Alas! I knew better!"

Q. "This 'strange light' on the night of 25th–26th January, 1938, astronomers call the Aurora Borealis. What do you think of it?"

A. "I think that if they examined the thing well, they would have perceived that, taking into account the circumstances under which this light appeared, it was not and could not have been an Aurora Borealis."

Q. "In the secret the Blessed Virgin says: 'To prevent that I shall come to ask for the consecration . . . and . . . the first Saturdays of the month.' Did she come?"

A. "Yes, she came into my room on December 10th, 1925, with the Infant Jesus, asking for the five first Saturdays of the month. . . Then in 1929, in the chapel at Tuy, she asked for the consecration . . ."

Q. "At what actual stage are we of the period mentioned in the secret?"

A. "I think that you are at that period when false doctrine shall propagate its errors throughout the world."

Someone spoke in the presence of Sister Lucy of the three beliefs of St. Grignon de Montfort, *viz.;* the reign of Jesus will come, by the reign of Mary, after the spreading throughout the world of the *True Devotion.* Sister Lucy reacted at once and added: "and after the conversion of Russia."

Fr. Fonseca's Comment

"We have given almost verbatim Lucy's words in this account of the greater part of the secret of Fatima, that is, that part which appears justified by events.

"Indeed, those who witnessed the horrors of the Spanish War (1936–'38), and who are aware of all that has happened since the beginning of the present war, need no comment in order to measure the importance of such a secret.

"However, it must be observed that the essential point in the secret is not the war, and its purpose is not the satisfaction of our curiosity, but the eternal salvation of souls. The secret reminded us, in short, of the great Catholic Truth: that *temporal evils are often manifestations of the Divine Justice provoked by the sins of men; and that they are at the same*

66

time a merciful call to repentance, without which these temporal misfortunes could become the terrible prelude to eternal evils. *It reminds us also of the necessity and efficacy of the intercession of the Most Blessed Virgin,* to obtain the Divine Mercy for us, for the Church and for all souls."

CHAPTER V

Commentary on the Secret by the Children Themselves

NOTHING shows up so forcibly the meaning and importance of the great secret of Fatima as the sayings and virtuous practices of the three children. They give us a lively appreciation of the inconceivable malice of sin, which offends God, causes the eternal loss of souls, grieves the motherly Heart of Mary and unlooses on the world the scourge of the Divine Justice.

The offence Against God

Several times in the course of these apparitions Our Lady of Fatima asked the three children to make reparation for the offences committed against the Divine Majesty, and in the message of October 13th, she begged sorrowfully: "Do not offend Our Lord any more. He is already offended too much." "What a loving reproach is contained in these words," writes Lucy, "what tender pleading! Oh! how I wish I could make them re-echo throughout the entire world, for all the children of our good Mother in heaven to hear!"

This same thought distressed little Jacinta. "Oh!" she cried shortly before her death, "the sins of the world are too great!"

Already the Angel had revealed to them that the Body and Blood of Our Lord Jesus Christ were horribly outraged by ungrateful men; and he had announced to them their sublime vocation saying: "Make reparation for their sins and console your God."

Console the Good God

The children understood this role of reparation and consolation in a special way, when they came to know God better, in that mysterious light which the heavenly Apparition cast on them.

·*Francis* seemed to be particularly gripped by the thought of God, and by the desire of consoling Him for the offence that sin causes Him. He often said to his companions: "We were all inflamed in the light which is God, and it did not burn us! Is it really God! We shall never be able to say! But what a pity it is that He is so sad! Ah! if only I could console Him!"

To console the Good God for the offence the sins of men cause Him, this became his dominant thought. "Francis," his companions asked him one day, "what are you doing, kneeling for such a long time?" *"I think* of the Good God who is so sad on account of so many sins! . . . Oh, how I wish I could console Him!" And for that reason he spent the afternoon in prayer refusing even to go for his lunch!

"I was very happy to see the Angel," he confided once to his companions, "more happy still to see the Blessed Virgin; but what made me happy above all was to see the Good God in this great light which the Blessed Virgin put in our breasts. I love the Good God so much! But how sad He is on account of so many sins! Oh, we must not sin again."

"Francis," Lucy asked one day: "which would you prefer: to console Our Divine Lord, or to convert sinners so that they may not go to hell?"

"I should rather console Our Lord! Did you not see how the Blessed Virgin became quite sad when she asked men not to offend Our Divine Lord any more, for He is already offended too much? . . . I should rather console Our Lord, and then convert sinners so that they may not offend Him again!"

Later, when he was already ill, he said again: "The Lord will be still so sad! *I offer Him,* for His consolation, *as many sacrifices as I can."*

Hell and Eternity

Jacinta showed herself more particularly moved by the thought of the eternity of hell. Even in the midst of a game, she would stop to ask Lucy: "Tell me: even after many, many, many years, hell will not end? . . . And these people who burn there, they do not die? . . . They are not reduced to ashes? . . . And if we *pray* very much for sinners, Our Lord will not send them to hell any more? And also if we *make sacrifices* for them? . . . Oh! the poor wretches! . . . How good the Blessed Virgin is to have promised us already to take us with her to heaven! . . ."

Often also did she sit, *wrapt in thought,* repeating wonderingly: "Hell! Hell! How they grieve me, those souls that go to hell! . . . These people still alive burn like wood in the fire!" And trembling with emotion she would throw herself on her knees, and joining her hands, repeat fervently: "O my Jesus, forgive us our sins, save us from the fire of hell, lead all souls to heaven, and help especially those who most need Your mercy."

Sometimes she would appear to arouse herself from a *profound meditation* and call her two companions: "Would you like to pray with me? We must pray very much to prevent souls from falling into hell. There are so many who fall! . . ."

Our holy Faith reveals to us the existence of hell, but many souls do not *meditate* enough on the eternal truths. Jacinta was distressed at this thought: "Ah!" she would say, "if sinners only saw what hell was like, as we have seen, they would sin no more, and would not go to hell! . . ."

And all engrossed by this *thought* she would repeat: "So many souls go to hell! So many! . . ."

"Do not be afraid," Lucy suggested to her one day, "you will go to heaven."

"I know that, the Blessed Virgin has promised us, but I would like all other souls to go there also! . . ."

And in order to help sinners to be converted and not fall into hell, *these generous children lived now only for prayers and heroic sacrifices,* whose detailed description sometimes brings tears to the eyes of those who read the beautiful account of their lives in *"Il était trois petits Enfants."*

The Sins of the World

Shortly before her death little Jacinta said sadly:

"The sins that lead most souls to hell are sins of the flesh! . . .

"Certain fashions will be introduced which will offend Our Divine Lord very much. Those who serve God ought not to follow these fashions. . .

"The sins of the world are too great! The Blessed Virgin has said that there will be many wars and disturbances in the world: *wars are only punishments for the sins of the world! . . .*

70

"The Blessed Virgin can no longer restrain the arm of her Divine Son, which will strike the world . . .

"Men must do penance . . . If they amend their lives, Our Lord will still forgive them; but if they do not reform, the punishment will surely come."

The Chastisement

Ill in bed, *Jacinta was thinking one day, holding her head in her hands,* when her mother asked: "What are you *thinking* about?" She only smiled, but later confided to Lucy: "I was *thinking* of Our Lord, of the Blessed Virgin, of sinners, and of the war that is to come . . . So many lives will be lost, and almost all will go to hell. So many houses will be destroyed, and so many priests will be killed.

"Oh! What a pity! If men ceased offending the Lord, the war would not come and such great numbers would not go to hell . . ."

The Sign in the Night

"Listen, Lucy," continued Jacinta, "I am going soon to heaven, (so I have nothing to fear from these chastisements). But you, when you see in the night that light which the Blessed Virgin mentioned, take refuge also above."

"But do you not see," replied Lucy, "that one cannot seek refuge like that in heaven? . . ."

"That is true . . . But still do not be afraid. In heaven I shall pray very much for you, and for the *Holy Father,* and for *Portugal* that the war may not come here, and *for all priests*".

The Holy Father

On another occasion Jacinta asked Lucy: "Have you seen the Holy Father? . . . I do not know how it happened, but I saw him in a very large house, kneeling before a little table, weeping, with his head between his hands. Outside there was a crowd. Some threw stones, others uttered curses and very wicked words . . . Poor Holy Father! . . ."

Two priests had one day recommended the little seers to pray for the Holy Father. Jacinta said afterwards to her companions: "It is he that I saw weeping, and of whom the Blessed Virgin spoke to us in the secret. Doubtless she has also shown him to these two priests. You see I was not mistaken. We must pray very much for him!"

We feel that in speaking about the Holy Father the children are still reticent. This is probably one of the things that belong to the third part of the secret which is still to be revealed. But the insistence of the children in praying for the Holy Father is significant. Offering Jesus their sacrifices, they added always: "*And for the Holy Father.*" After their Rosary they never failed to add three *Hail Marys* for the Holy Father, and they always exhorted one another to pray very much for him.

Prayers for the Holy Father have since become traditional in the Sanctuary of Fatima, whence this truly Catholic devotion has spread throughout the whole country so much that on May 13th, 1942, His Lordship the Bishop of Leiria has been able to rejoice in the fact that *"Fatima has created in Portugal devotion to the Pope".*

May the example of Fatima awaken in all Christians this filial devotion towards the Vicar of Jesus Christ, whom St. Catherine of Ciena called respectfully: "The Sweet Christ on Earth."

CHAPTER VI

The Triple Message of Fatima: Penance, Rosary, Devotion to the Immaculate Heart of Mary

FOR the proper understanding of the great fact of Fatima two things must be carefully distinguished: the *prodigies,* and the *message* of the Blessed Virgin.

The Message or recommendations of Our Lady of the Rosary of Fatima constitute the *end* or object of these apparitions. The prodigies, on the contrary, are only a *means* of proving undeniably the heavenly origin of the message.

Doubtless, what strikes us most at first in the great events of Fatima are the incomparable solar prodigies, which are truly unique in the history of the world, and which awaken our dormant faith. *But the important thing above all for us to remember, to put carefully into practice, and to spread around us, is the message of the recommendations of Our Lady of Fatima.*

Until quite recently this message was known only from the few words of the apparition on October 13th, 1917. But the recent official publications enable us to understand it better by showing clearly the occasion, the purpose and the interrelations of these great apparitions at Cova da Iria.

Though a portion of the "Secret" still remains hidden, it is nevertheless possible to trace the *connection of the events of Fatima!*

The sins of the modern world have become too great. Men stupidly deify the flesh, and coldly refuse to recognise Jesus Christ and His Church, God and His laws. As in the time of Noah man's malice had cried to heaven for vengeance and brought the deluge upon the earth, so the sins of the modern world have finally provoked the Divine Justice, which decided to drown this wicked world in a new deluge of blood and fire—the First World War.

Moved with pity the Blessed Virgin interceded with her Divine Son, and obtained from the Divine Mercy a truce, a postponement of the chastisement.

In spite of the wonderful prodigies which accompanied them, this heavenly counsel was not sufficiently heeded, and the Divine Justice resumed its course in a war still more terrible—the Second World War.

But God is infinitely good, and the Blessed Virgin tireless in her merciful intercessions. *If men wake up, and listen even now to the heavenly message of the Immaculate Heart of Mary, the chastisement, which has not been completely avoided, could at least be mitigated.* This is what *Cardinal Schuster of Milan* recalled in his pastoral letter of 1942, basing his statement on the authentic documents: *"If we comply faithfully with these demands,"* he wrote, *"Our Lady of Fatima promises us peace, the return of Russia to the Catholic unity, and the beginning of a new era of apostolate and conquest for the Catholic Church."*

In the next three chapters therefore we shall set forth the triple request of Our Lady of Fatima: penance, the Rosary, and devotion to the Immaculate Heart of Mary. Let us study lovingly this threefold message of Fatima, let us put it faithfully into practice and let us spread it around us. We could not help more efficaciously in drawing on the poor world the blessing of God.

CHAPTER VII

Penance

ALREADY, in the preparatory apparitions of 1916, the Angel of Fatima had asked for prayers and sacrifices in reparation for the sins of the world and to obtain the conversion of sinners. The Blessed Virgin in all her apparitions repeated the same request under different forms. Finally, on October 13th, 1917, she insisted a last time saying: "Men must amend their lives, and ask pardon for their sins." Then with a more sorrowful air and with a suppliant voice she added: "Men must no longer offend Our Lord, Who is already offended too much."

Such is the Message of Penance of Fatima! It asks us not only to repent for our past sins and to expiate them faithfully, but also to change our lives for the future and to break completely with sin, which grieves God and draws down on us His chastisement.

Commenting on this Message of Penance, Lucy writes with emotion: "The part of this last apparition which has remained *most deeply imprinted* on my heart is the prayer of our heavenly Mother begging us *not to offend any more Almighty God,* Who is already very much offended. What a loving reproach is contained in these words, what tender pleading! Oh! I wish I could make it re-echo throughout the entire world for all the children of our heavenly Mother to hear!"

No less touching is Jacinta's comment in February, 1920, shortly before her death. With what ardour did not this child of ten preach amendment of life, not only to sinners, but also to faithful souls! How she insisted on flight from sin, the practice of the Christian virtues and penance!

"Oh!" she said to the Superioress of the Orphanage in Lisbon, "if men only knew what eternity is, how they would make all possible efforts to amend their lives! Dear Godmother (this is how she addressed the Superioress), mortification and sacrifice give great pleasure to Our Divine Lord! Oh! fly luxury! Fly riches! Love holy poverty! Be very charitable even towards the wicked! Never speak evil of anyone and avoid those who do. Be very patient because patience leads to heaven.

"Pray much for sinners! Pray much for priests, for Religious, for Governments! Priests should occupy themselves only with the affairs of the Church! They must be pure, very pure. The disobedience of priests and of religious to their Superiors and to the Holy Father offends Our Lord very much! If Governments left the Church in peace and gave liberty to our holy religion, they would be blessed by God.

"The sins of the world are too great! The sins which lead most souls to hell are sins of the flesh! . . . Oh! Men must do penance! If they amend their lives Our Lord will still pardon the world; but if they do not, the chastisement will come! . . ."

It would appear that in announcing these things the *Blessed Virgin was very sad,* for Jacinta added: "The poor Blessed Virgin! I pity her so much, so much! . . ."

Recording these words of Jacinta in February, 1920, the Superioress added the following note: "This refers to a great punishment of which the child spoke to me confidentially. May God have mercy on us! In a few years many things will be seen in the world! The Blessed Virgin said, it is true, 'If men do not amend their lives!' So it depends on us. God have mercy on us!"

How eloquent do these words written in 1920 become when read to-day . . .

Let us then give a loving welcome to the message of penance of Our Lady of Fatima! Let us acknowledge humbly that we have all merited the just chastisement of God. Let us sincerely ask pardon for our past sins, and with the help of grace, let us set ourselves seriously to the task of reforming our lives.

Let *sinners* amend their lives and become good Christians by the constant observance of God's law. Let the *good* also amend their lives and strive to become better each day. Let the *better* change and apply themselves ardently to becoming perfect.

Let even the *perfect* change their lives, and aspire with all their souls to that elevated sanctity which consoles God and averts from the world its just chastisements! . . .

We admit that it is always foolish to offend God, but it would be a crime still more unintelligible to provoke the Divine anger at a time when the world is afflicted with so much misery and is confronted by so many grave problems. Nay more! the Pope has assured us that the thunderbolt of Divine Justice will strike once again, unless we amend our lives. Let us then renounce resolutely, in a spirit of penance, all indulgence, all sensuality! In a depraved world gone mad, which continues to seek amusement and dissipation and debases itself with evil, *let us prove ourselves true Christians who understand the meaning of the fearful trial through which we are passing,* who sanctify their sufferings and do all in their power to merit the pardon and blessing of God.

Let us remember the inhabitants of Nineveh! Let us, like them, sincerely do penance for our sins, and then will happen to us what the Holy Schipture says of them: *"God saw that they had turned away from their evil ways! He had mercy with regard to the evil which He had promised to do them, and did not do it!"* Our Lady of the Rosary of Fatima, pray for us!

CHAPTER VIII

The Rosary

BESIDES being a message of penance, *Fatima is also par excellence "The Message of the Rosary"*. Indeed it is about the Rosary that the great events of Fatima have unfolded themselves; and on October 13th, the heavenly vision formally declared herself "Our Lady of the Rosary."

The Rosary, Centre of the Apparitions

On Sunday, May 13th, 1917, the midday angelus is heard from the tower of Fatima, and the three little children, trained by truly Christian parents, leave their play of their own accord, to recite the Rosary together. It is at that moment that the "Lady" appears to them as if in approval of their prayer. She herself has the Rosary hanging from her waist; she makes Francis recite the Rosary that he may see her on the tree, and tells him that he must recite many Rosaries to enter heaven. Finally, before retiring, the heavenly Lady makes this recommendation: "Continue, my children, reciting the Rosary with devotion, every day, to obtain peace for the world."

On Wednesday, June 13th, the three children await the apparition reciting the Rosary with the people: and the heavenly Lady recommends them a second time to recite the Rosary every day.

On Friday, July 13th, it is with a crowd of from four to five thousand people that the little seers recite the Rosary at Cova da Iria. The apparition insists a third time:

"You must recite the Rosary every day in honour of Our Lady of the Rosary to obtain peace for the world and the end of the war, for only she can obtain this."

And then she promises the great miracle for October 13th, "in order that the world may believe" that it is indeed she who speaks. At the same time the Blessed Virgin promises to heal sick people recommended to her, but on condition that they recite the Rosary to that end. She even asks the cripple of Atouguia to recite the *family Rosary*.

It is also during this apparition that Lucy is heard to repeat, as if to retain well what the Lady has first recommended to her: "Yes, she wishes people to recite the Rosary, people must recite the Rosary . . ."

After the "great Secret", the Blessed Virgin comes back once more to the Rosary, and asks them to add at the end of each decade the short prayer: "O Jesus forgive us our sins, save us from the fire of hell, and lead all souls to heaven especially those who have most need of Your mercy!"

On Sunday, August 19th, the apparition insists again: "You must recite the Rosary every day," and exhort the little ones to pray very much and to offer sacrifices for poor sinners, many of whom fall into hell because there is nobody to pray or to offer sacrifices for them!

On Thursday, September 13th, the three children recite the Rosary again with the thirty thousand pilgrims present: and the Blessed Virgin repeats once more: "You must continue to recite the Rosary in honour of Our Lady of the Rosary, in order that she may put an end to the war!"

Finally, on October 13th, all the requests made previously about the Rosary are repeated once more in the words of the Message and by means of the multiple apparition beside the sun. In fact, in the Message of Fatima the heavenly apparition declares to the world that she is Our Lady of the Rosary come down to earth in person to exhort men to *amend their lives and to say the Rosary every day!*

In the multiple apparition that took place during the great solar prodigy, it is the mysteries of the Rosary that Our Lady of Fatima recommends to us under the concrete form of the "tableaux vivants". The first scene of The Holy Family, says Fr. Fonseca, represents to us the joyful mysteries of the Infancy of Jesus. The scene of Our Lady of the Seven Dolours recalls to our minds the Sorrowful Mysteries and exhorts us to do penance. Lastly, Our Lady of Mount Carmel, with the Sabbatine privilege, reminds us of the Glorious Mysteries and of our last end, and exhorts us to avoid hell, to live for heaven and to shorten as much as possible the expiation of purgatory.

The Rosary, Centre of the Message

It can therefore be said in all truth, that if the Message of Fatima comprises a threefold object: penance, the Rosary, and the Immaculate Heart of Mary, *it is the Rosary that forms the central point.*

This is exactly how little Jacinta summarised the Message of Fatima to someone who asked her: "What Our Lady of the Rosary especially recommended to us is to recite the Rosary every day, adding after each decade the short prayer: O my Jesus forgive us our sins, save us from the fire of Hell, lead all souls to heaven, and help especially those who most need your mercy." Dr. Formigan, who was the first to follow closely the entire course of the events of Fatima, writes in his turn: "The Message of Fatima can be summed up in two words: "Rosary and Expiation!"

To recite the Rosary devoutly every day, with sincere feelings of penance and reparation: *Such is the substance and the core of the heavenly Message of Fatima.*

"I am Our Lady of the Rosary"

Our Lady of the Rosary had already appeared previously to St. Dominic, charging him to preach the great devotion of the Rosary as an efficacious remedy for the regeneration of souls and as a powerful means of obtaining heavenly succour in public misfortunes. It is through the Rosary that Our Lady has come to the help of the Church and of Society during the critical periods of the Albigensian heresy and the Turkish invasions. And it is by this same simple means that Our Lady of Fatima wishes to-day to reform souls and to save the world from the awful calamities that overwhelm it.

The devout and constant recitation of the Rosary always works miracles. It tires neither the lips that recite it nor the heart that loves; but it finally tires God Who, importuned by Our Lady, grants at last the graces requested.

The Rosary is a treasury of prayer upon which the learned and ignorant can draw, to offer to God and the Blessed Virgin their tribute of homage and their share of penance and expiation.

The Rosary can be recited everywhere, and can be joined to all other devotions. The labourer recites it going in the morning to his daily work; the domestic servant says it on the road while executing her commissions; the artisan in his workshop while his hands work, the traveller on the train and the nurse at the bedside of her patients. The sick person assuages his pains by telling the beads in his feeble fingers; the dying lovingly kisses his Rosary and asks to have it entwined round his hands after death, as a sign of his confidence in Mary and a pledge of the divine mercy. And all, as by a permanent miracle, feel strengthened, consoled and reassured.

The Rosary is a mark of Predestination. The mother, who on her deathbed makes her children promise to say the Rosary every day, can die in peace. She feels she is sure to find them all again one day beside her in heaven.

"The Rosary," said Fr. Vaysière, "is not a devotion to the Blessed Virgin, it is *the* devotion to Mary!" Let us then, like the little seers of Fatima and all the saints, learn to appreciate the immense value of the Rosary, which the Blessed Virgin recommends to us so strongly.

The Little Seers and the Rosary

On May 13th, the apparition had promised Francis that he would go to heaven on condition that he recited many Rosaries. On learning this piece of good news from his companions,[1] the little shepherd boy became quite radiant with joy! Crossing his hands on his breast and raising his eyes to heaven, he cried lovingly: "Oh! Blessed Virgin! Rosaries! I shall say as many of them as you want!"

The three children usually said several Rosaries together every day; but Francis added others in private. Often he would leave off playing with his companions and walk about in silence.

"What are you doing Francis?" they asked him one day. In answer, he showed them his Rosary.

"Come and play with us a little; afterwards we shall all pray together!"

"After? I must pray both now and afterwards," replied this

---

[1] Francis saw the apparition, but did not hear it.

young boy of nine. "Do you not remember what Our Lady said, that I must recite many Rosaries?"

Indeed he said as many as eight or nine Rosaries a day, without speaking of the long hours spent in reciting the Angel's prayers.

His little companions showed themselves no less ardent in offering each day to their heavenly Mother many fervent Rosaries.

One is moved on seeing the loving care that the Blessed Virgin took in thus training them. On May 9th, 1918, during the Mass of the Ascension, little Jacinto again received a visit from Our Lady of Fatima, who had maternally undertaken to teach her to recite the Rosary well, meditating lovingly on the mysteries.

Must not the Rosary, then, have a special importance and power, for Our Lady of Fatima, after recommending it so insistently and calling herself "The Lady of the Rosary," to have yet taken the pains of coming herself to teach these little seers how to recite it well? Besides, since the time of St. Dominic all the Saints have had a singular love for the Rosary. Let us give a few examples.

The Saints and the Rosary

Saint Dominic, who had received the revelation of the Rosary, said in a sermon: "After the Divine Office and the Holy Mass, no homage is as agreeable to Jesus and His divine Mother as the fervent recitation of the Rosary!" And to confirm this truth he worked a miracle!

Saint Bernard loved to say that "the *Hail Mary* puts the devil to flight, and causes hell to tremble with terror!"

Pope Saint Pius V recited the Rosary every day. Before the decisive Battle of Lepanto he requested that the Rosary be recited throughout all Christendom to obtain victory; and he caused a Rosary to be given to each soldier as the best of arms. The victory of the Christians over the Turks was overwhelming!

Saint Charles Borromeo called the Rosary "the most divine of prayers after the Holy Sacrifice of the Mass." Not only did he recite it every day kneeling with his household, but he imposed it on all his seminarists, and recommended it to all his clergy in this imperative formula: "You shall recite the Rosary, as often as you are able."

Saint Louis de Montfort said: "It has always been observed that those who bear the mark of reprobation, like the heretics, the impious, the proud, hate or despise the *Hail Mary* and the Rosary". And he added: "I find nothing more powerful in drawing within us the Kingdom of God, the Eternal Wisdom, than to join vocal to mental prayer by reciting the holy Rosary and meditating on the fifteen mysteries".

Saint John Chrysostom said: "God governs the world, but prayer governs God Himself!"

Saint Alphonsus often repeated, and Pius XII recalled it in July, 1941: "He who prays, is saved; he who prays not, is damned!"

The Cure d'Ars in his turn, said with emotion: "I know something stronger than God: the man who prays. He makes God say: 'Yes', when He had said 'No!' "

Saint Francis de Sales added: "The best method of prayer is the Rosary, if you say it well." Add up the evidence of these sayings, and you will have an idea of the value of the holy Rosary! The same Saint loved to say that if he was not bound to the Office, he would recite no other prayer than the Rosary. He added: "To say my Rosary is the most pleasant occupation and the most pure joy of my heart." And St. Jeanne de Chantal informs us that she bound herself to recite the whole Rosary every day and spent an hour at it.

Father Lamy, apostle of the Red suburb of Paris, always had his Rosary in his hand. "When you go about saying the Rosary", he said, "you have nothing to fear! It is the recitation of the Rosary that makes Lucifer desperate. He is the sworn enemy of the Rosary. *Even if I had not the love of God, I should recite the Rosary just to annoy him!*"

The Holy Cure d'Ars one day caused a tremor to pass through his audience by declaring: "If, in order to give something to the Blessed Virgin I could sell myself, I should do so!" Without having to sell ourselves we can give our Rosary every day to the Blessed Virgin who asks us for it. Let us then not fail to do so, to show her our love, and to draw her blessing on ourselves and on this poor wretched world.

The Church and the Rosary

We should never end were we to quote all the praises the saints give to the Rosary. But let us now hear what Holy Church herself says of it, through the voice of the Sovereign Pontiffs.

First in a general way, it is truly impressive to find that since Our Lady revealed the Rosary to St. Dominic, *more than fifty Popes* have raised their voices to repeat to the whole Church with pressing insistence: "The Rosary is of divine rather than human origin; it is the prayer most agreeable to Mary: it contains in itself all the honour owed to Mary: it is the best means of obtaining her protection and her favours; it is the most efficacious means of satisfying for offences against the divine Majesty and for healing the deplorable evils which ruin the individual, the family and Society." Here are some words of the Popes of recent times:

Gregory XVI says that the Rosary "is the most wonderful means of destroying sin and recovering the grace of God."

Pius IX, amidst the great sorrows of his pontificate, wrote: "We are filled with joy at the thought that Our Lady will destroy as she has in times past, the monstrous errors of our century and that she will be able to thwart the sacrilegious attack of the wicked, on condition that all the faithful often recite the holy Rosary." The same Pope added in 1877: *"Great is the strength of an army that holds in its hands, not the sword but the Rosary."*

But it is Leo XIII above all, the successor of Pius IX, who has repeatedly explained to the whole Church the supreme importance of the holy Rosary, with an insistence so pressing and constant that he has been called: *"The Pope of the Rosary".*

From the Vatican hill where he was then a prisoner, the great Pontiff saw rising more and more the impetuous torrent of error and modern revolt, which, after misleading so many souls, finally threatened to bear away to its ruin society itself. Like Our Lord in the Agony at Gethsemani, Leo XIII prolonged his prayer. Then suddenly, his soul was as it were, raised up. Is it by a simple divine instinct, or by an express revelation of the "Queen of the Holy Rosary"? Perhaps history will tell us some day. But the eyes of this "Christ on Earth", till then sorrowful, were raised with unspeakable confidence towards the mysterious Woman of the Apocalypse, whose co-redemptive dolours brought forth the world to life. His prayer ascended in supplication to the Virgin of the Rosary, the Virgin of the mysteries of Christ, of all the mysteries: of joy, of redeeming sorrow, and of final triumph of the Crucified Victor over hell.

On September 1st, 1883, Leo XIII issued an encyclical ordering that, throughout the entire Catholic Church, the month of October of that year be consecrated to the *devotion of the holy Rosary,* and granted indulgences to this end. On December 24th of the same year, he asked insistently in a Brief that the Rosary become a daily practice; and he ordered to be added to the litanies the invocation: *"Queen of the Most Holy Rosary, pray for us."*

In 1884 he issued a new encyclical on the holy Rosary.

In 1885 another encyclical promulgated the Holy Year and ordered penance and the Rosary to be preached everywhere. In *1886,* in a letter to the Cardinal Vicar, Leo XIII insisted again on the devotion of the Rosary and ordered its recitation *every day of the year* in the churches of Rome dedicated to the Blessed Virgin.

In 1887 appeared a new letter to the Bishops of Italy on the month of October and the holy Rosary. *In 1889* he sent another encyclical to the entire Church. "The hour is critical", said he, "Let us pray through the Rosary, and let us add the *prayer to St. Joseph."* Then encyclicals *follow one another each year* on the same subject of the holy Rosary: in *1891* a new encyclical on the Rosary, in *1892* another, in *1893* still another, and so on in *1894, 1895* and *1896. In 1897* Leo XIII comes back again on the Rosary with special delight. Recalling what God has done to honour Mary, he adds with emotion: *"As Vicar of Jesus Christ, I wish also to honour Our Lady of the Rosary, and say to each Christian 'Behold Thy Mother.' "* Then he recommends with redoubled insistence *the Confraternity of the Rosary and the Perpetual Rosary.*

In 1898 Leo XIII insists again on the recitation of the Rosary. He summarises all that he has said on this subject in his many encyclicals, and grants *numerous indulgences* to this holy exercise.

Finally, on September 8th, 1901, appears yet another apostolic letter on the holy Rosary, on the occasion of the consecration of the new Basilica of the Rosary at Lourdes.

It is unique in the annals of the Church to see the same Pope speaking to the faithful on one single subject—the holy Rosary—in twelve encyclicals and almost as many decrees and apostolic constitutions! And if this golden chain of pontifical documents on the Rosary has been interrupted, it is because the holy Pontiff died! . . .

Let us read with respect and love all these masterly encyclicals of Leo XIII and ask heaven for *the grace to grasp fully the supreme importance of the holy Rosary, that the "Christ on Earth" has preached to us with such insistence,* "as the providential remedy for all the evils of our time!"

Pius X had no longer to insist on this teaching which his predecessor Leo XIII had developed in such masterly fashion. But a large part of his *testament* is consecrated to the holy Rosary. This is what he says:

"The Rosary is the most beautiful and the most rich in graces of all prayers, it is the prayer that touches most the Heart of the Mother of God . . . and if you wish peace to reign in your homes, recite the family Rosary".

Pius XI had also consecrated to the Rosary his encyclical of September 29th, 1937, in which he says: "The holy Rosary occupies a special and *exceptional* place among the various public prayers we address to the Virgin Mother of God".

Fatima Confirms the Voice of the Popes

In support of such weighty authorities comes finally the wonderful *event of Fatima*. Consider the account of the apparitions of Fatima with their words and prodigies. Recall especially the great day of the Rosary of Fatima and the incomparable solar prodigy. As in time past Almighty God promulgated *the law of Moses on Mount Sinai* amidst thunder and lightning and a holy terror of souls, so might we say the Blessed Virgin has willed to *promulgate the law of the holy Rosary on the mountain of Fatima* with an extraordinary abundance of external signs and prodigies which have produced in hearts sincere contrition.

Fatima is, as it were, a new and solemn promulgation of the immortal encyclicals of Leo XIII on the Rosary, which the heavenly apparition has thus confirmed and recommended to the entire world by incomparable prodigies!

Furthermore, in view of the prolongation of the evils of the world war and the imminent dangers from the impious atheistic movement which was then being organised, *Pope Benedict XV* had decided to mobilize the Catholic Church in a campaign of prayer, to obtain peace for the world through the intercession of the Blessed Virgin. He wrote to Cardinal Gasparri: "Since all graces are distributed to us through the hands of the Blessed Virgin, now in this terrible hour we wish more than ever that the prayers of Mary's afflicted children be directed with lively confidence to the august Mother of God. We therefore charge you to make known to the Bishops of the entire world our ardent desire that recourse be had to this throne through Mary". At the same time the Sovereign Pontiff ordered to be added to the litanies the invocation: "Queen of Peace, pray for us."

This letter of Benedict XV, dated Saturday, May 5th, 1917, and made public some days later, had hardly been published by the press of the various countries, when on Sunday, May 13th, Our Lady of the Rosary appeared at Fatima, and during her apparitions, asked for the "recitation of the Rosary to obtain the end of the war," adding "that she alone could come to our aid."

It was clearly the voice of heaven answering the voice of the Vicar of Jesus Christ. He had just invited the entire world to ask God for peace through the intercession of Mary. The Blessed Virgin came to make clear that she alone indeed could help us to bring to an end the great scourge of war, and that this grace must be sought through the Rosary, recited with feelings of sincere contrition and penance.

The Portuguese people have remained faithful to the Message of Our Lady of the Rosary of Fatima. Faith has been re-awakened in souls, and *the Rosary has become, in Portugal, the great daily prayer of individuals and families*. Besides, this small country which for many years lived in a habitual state of agitation and violent upheavals—in sixteen years it had seen sixteen revolutions, eight presidents of the Republic, forty-three changes of ministry, and financial disaster!—this country has ended by finding, once more, after the great events at Fatima, peace and prosperity.

May the great solar prodigy of Fatima revive faith in souls everywhere, and bring men to realise in a practical manner that *the heavenly Message of Our Lady of the Rosary is the condition laid down by God for coming out of the chaos in which the world is struggling.*

"Our Lady of the Rosary of Fatima, pray for us!"

CHAPTER IX

The Immaculate Heart of Mary

FATIMA is, in the third place, the message of devotion to the Immaculate Heart of Mary.

It will be remembered that already in the preparatory apparitions of 1916, the "Angel of Peace" had united the holy hearts of Jesus and Mary, when speaking of the designs of mercy that would soon be fulfilled in the three little seers. Our Lady of Fatima also, from *her first apparition* in 1917, asked for reparation for all the blasphemies and offences against the Immaculate Heart of Mary.

At the second apparition on June 13th, Our Lady of Fatima said to Lucy: "You must remain longer on earth. Jesus wishes to use you in making me known and loved. *He wishes to spread in the world the devotion to my Immaculate Heart.* I promise salvation to those who embrace this devotion. *Their souls will be loved by God with a love of predilection,* like flowers placed by me before His throne!" When Lucy appeared sad at the thought of remaining alone on earth after the death of her two companions, Our Lady said: "No, my child, I shall never abandon you. My Immaculate Heart will be your refuge and the way that will lead you to God."

A reading of the account of *the third apparition,* completed by that of the secret of Fatima, will quickly show that devotion to the Immaculate Heart of Mary holds an important place in the Message. After the terrifying vision of the loss of souls, Our Lady of Fatima said: "You have just seen hell where poor sinners go. *To save them the Lord wishes to establish in the world the devotion of my Immaculate Heart.* If people do what I shall tell you, many souls will be saved, and there will be peace. The war (1914–18) is coming to an end. But if men do not cease offending the Lord, a worse war will begin in the reign of Pope Pius XI".

She added: ". . . I shall ask for the consecration of Russia to *my Immaculate Heart,* as well as communion of reparation on the first Saturday of the month. *If my requests are granted, Russia will be converted and there will be peace.* Otherwise Russia will spread its errors through the world, raising up wars and persecutions against the Church. The good will be martyred, the Holy Father will have to suffer much, several nations will be wiped out . . ."

There are reticences in these official documents. The competent authority still observes great reserve in these publications, so as not to terrify our weak nature, so gloomy is the perspective of the chastisement provoked by our sins! Nevertheless, even if Society were to come to a period of disorganisation and chaos, we must never give way to despair. A consoling word of Our Lady of Fatima should fill us with confidence throughout: *"My Immaculate Heart will finally triumph."*

When and how will this triumph take place? "That", says Fr Fonseca, "is the part of the 'Secret' that will be more clearly revealed in its proper time. In the meantime we are given to understand that the consecration to the Immaculate Heart of Mary requested by the Blessed Virgin will be made; that as a result of this consecration *Russia will be converted to Catholicism and a certain period of peace will be granted to the world; that Portugal will have the happiness of preserving the gift of the Faith, etc. . ."*

Therefore since July 13th, 1917, Our Lady of the Rosary of Fatima presented to us the devotion to her Immaculate Heart, and especially the practice of the First Saturdays and the consecration to her Immaculate Heart, as the providential means offered to the modern world, not only of ensuring the salvation of a large number of souls, but also of preserving or giving back peace to the world.

The New Apparitions

After 1917, says Fr Fonseca in his sixth edition, new apparitions, entirely intimate, came to complete the previous revelations, making more precise especially the practical way of making raparation and the consecration to the Immaculate Heart of Mary.

As we cannot give all these revelations, it will be sufficient to say for the present, that on December 10th, 1925, the Blessed Virgin with the Infant Jesus beside her, appeared again to Lucy, the sole survivor of the little seers of Fatima. She showed her Immaculate Heart surrounded with thorns; and the *Infant Jesus* said, indicating it with His hands: *"Have pity on this loving Heart, a continual martyr to the ingratitude of men."* The Blessed Virgin added: "See, my child, this Heart of mine, surrounded with the thorns with which men transfix it at every moment by their blasphemy and ingratitude. Do you at least try to console me, and announce in my name that I promise to assist at the hour of death with the graces necessary for salvation, all those who, on the *first Saturday of five consecutive months, go to confession and receive Holy Communion, recite the Rosary, and keep me company for a quarter of an hour while meditating on the mysteries of the Rosary, with the intention of making reparation".*

Two months later, on February 15th, 1926, *the Infant Jesus again appeared to Lucy, encouraging her to spread the devotion to the Immaculate Heart of Mary,* and not to allow herself to be stopped by the difficulties pointed out by confessors, because with God's help they would be easily overcome. Taking advantage of the opportunity, Lucy asked if confession made during the week would count for the first Saturday of the month. The reply was it would; but it is to be understood that Communion must be received in the state of grace and with the intention of making reparation as indicated above.

The Children's Comments

Lucy relates that on June 13th, 1917, after speaking at length about her Immaculate Heart, Our Lady of Fatima again stretched forth her hands, throwing on the children the rays of that immense light in which they saw themselves as if immersed in God . . . The Blessed Virgin held in her right hand *a Heart surrounded by thorns, which pierced it from all sides.* The seers understood that it was the Immaculate Heart of Mary, afflicted by all the sins of the world, which demanded penance and reparation. "It seems to me," said Lucy, "that on that day, the purpose of the light was to pour into us a special knowledge and love of the Immaculate Heart of Mary, as on other occasions it infused into us the knowledge and love of God, and the mystery of the Blessed Trinity. From that day, indeed, we experienced a more ardent love for the Immaculate Heart of Mary."

Francis had observed that this supernatural light, that the Blessed Virgin threw on them and on the world, *seemed to come from her Heart.* He afterwards asked Lucy: "Why did the Blessed Virgin hold a Heart in her hand throwing on the earth this great light which is God? You were with the Blessed Virgin in the light that went down to the earth, while Jacinta and I were in that which went up to heaven!"

"It is because you and Jacinta will soon go to heaven", said Lucy, "while I shall remain some time longer on earth with the Immaculate Heart of Mary".

"Is it the Blessed Virgin who explained to you the meaning of the two beams of light?"

"No, I saw it in the light that she put into our breasts."

"That is right", interposed Jacinta, who followed the conversation, "I saw it also".

Jacinta seems to have received "a special light to understand intimately and in detail the meanings of these heavenly revelations". Before leaving for hospital in 1919, she said to Lucy: "I am going soon to heaven. You will remain still on earth to make known to men that the Lord wishes to spread in the world devotion to the Immaculate Heart of Mary. When you have to speak about it, you will no longer have to hide yourself! Proclaim openly to the whole world that:

"**It is through the Immaculate Heart of Mary that God wishes to grant us His graces!**"

"**It is from this Immaculate Heart that we must ask for them!**"

"**The Heart of Jesus wishes the Immaculate Heart of Mary to be venerated with His own!**"

"**It is through the Immaculate Heart of Mary that peace must be asked, because it is to that Heart that the Lord has confided it.**"

"**How I love the Immaculate Heart of Mary! It is the Heart of Our Heavenly Mother!**"

"**Oh! if only I could put into all hearts the fire I feel in my own, which makes me love the Hearts of Jesus and Mary so much!**"

Besides, the best commentary on the devotion to the Immaculate Heart of Mary is that left us by the children in the admirable example of their lives. After the revelations, indeed, they were true models of devotion and reparation to the Immaculate Heart of Mary. They loved this Immaculate Heart ardently, they invoked it constantly, they spoke about it enthusiastically, and they multiplied sacrifices to console it and to make reparation for all the blasphemies and offences that cause it to suffer.

Practices of Devotion to the Immaculate Heart

We have already spoken of penance and the daily Rosary so much recommended by Our Lady of Fatima. We give now the three principal practices of devotion for which she has asked in honour of her Immaculate Heart; the First Saturday of the month, the Five First Saturdays and the Consecration. They bear a marked similarity to the practices now so widespread in honour of the Sacred Heart of Jesus.

1. *The practice of the First Saturdays consists of* the following exercises, *performed with the intention of consoling the Immaculate Heart of Mary,* and making reparation to it for all the outrages and blasphemies of which it is the object on the part of ungrateful Christians: 1, the Rosary; 2, Communion of Reparation.

2. *For the practice of the Five First Saturdays.* In addition to the two exercises already mentioned, the following two are added on the first Saturday of five consecutive months: 3, go to confession; 4, keep the company of the Immaculate Heart of Mary by *meditating* for a quarter of an hour on the mysteries of the Rosary. These two must be offered *in reparation* to the Immaculate Heart.

Practical Remarks: Confession during the week, for the First Friday for instance, counts for the first Saturday, or conversely when the Saturday is the first day of the month. The meditation may be on one or several mysteries. It is recommended that we meditate each month on a different mystery, so that by performing the devotion of the Five Saturdays three times, the fifteen mysteries of the Rosary would be considered.

3. *Consecration to the Immaculate Heart of Mary.* As is known, Our Lady asked that Russia be consecrated to her Immaculate Heart and Lucia, the surviving seer has explained that She wants the Pope and all the bishops of the world to do this on one special day. If this is done She will convert Russia and there will be peace. The journalist William Thomas Walsh quoted her verbatim as saying ". . . if it is not done the errors of Russia will spread through every country in the world." Walsh's interview with Lucia took place in 1946.

On October 31st, 1942, on the occasion of the closing of the Jubilee Celebrations at Fatima, the Sovereign Pontiff, Pope

Pius XII, consecrated officially to the Immaculate Heart of Mary, the Church, the world and Russia in particular. Then on December 8th of the same year, in the Basilica of St. Peter, he renewed this consecration with the greatest solemnity. To emphasize the sovereign importance which he attached to this consecration, His Holiness ordered that the annual medal struck to commemorate the most prominent event of the year, should be dedicated that year to commemorate the consecration of the world and Russia to the Immaculate Heart of Mary. Finally, Pope Pius XII granted to the Universal Church the Feast of the Immaculate Heart of Mary, with proper Mass Office.

The first and most essential step has been taken. But there are others equally important, which we must take if we wish to gather in abundance all the promised fruits, because the grace of God, to be effective, requires our own cooperation.

To this solemn act performed by the Holy Father *in the name of all, we should then give its natural complement by our consecration,* both individual and collective. Let us enter wholeheartedly into this great Catholic movement, and let us be happy to consecrate to the Immaculate Heart of Mary, our persons, our families, our works, our country, all our interests spiritual and temporal. We shall then be sure of doing something pleasing to Our Heavenly Mother, and of drawing her blessings of peace and salvation on ourselves and on the whole world.

But the consecration asked by Our Lady of Fatima does not consist solely in the recitation of a formula. *It should be for us a real programme of Christian life,* accompanied by a solemn resolution of putting it into practce under the maternal protection of the Immaculate Heart of Mary.

Let us bear in mind the recent example of Portugal, that Our Lady of Fatima has lifted up from its ruins, to make of it in a few years a happy country, respected by the entire world. If, amid all our misfortunes, we accept the heavenly message of Fatima and consecrate ourselves to the Immaculate Heart of Mary, living in a manner worthy of our consecration, we may be sure that our salvation will be certain, glorious, and lasting.

A Future of Hope

Cardinal Cerejeira, Patriarch of Lisbon, preaching at Fatima during the Jubilee Celebration of March 13th, 1942, said: "Our Lady of the Rosary came down at Fatima, bringing to the world *a message whose importance cannot even yet be measured*. This fact opens up bright horizons of hope in the gloomy mist of the present. With great hope we have confidence that through the intercession of the Immaculate Heart of Mary whom we call the Mother of Mercy, God is preparing great things for the world. . . Many might be tempted to expect the approach of the end of the world. Why not rather think, since we believe in Providence and in the maternal Heart of the Immaculate Virgin, that it is the painful birth of a new world? . . .

"Fatima has not yet told Portugal and the world all its secret; but it does not appear to us too much to say that *what it has already revealed to Portugal is the sign and the earnest of what it has in store for the world!*"

The same eminent Prelate wrote in the preface to the Life of Jacinta (October, 1942):

"We believe that the apparitions of Fatima open a new era, that of the Immaculate Heart of Mary. What has taken place in Portugal is of the miraculous order. It is the foreshadowing of what the Immaculate Heart of Mary is preparing for the world!"

PART III

THE PILGRIMAGE

CHAPTER I

The Effect of the Great Solar Prodigy

THE news of the Great Prodigy of Fatima, spread by telegraph, newspaper and by the innumerable eye-witnesses of this extraordinary event, flashed across the whole of Portugal.[1] *The effect was prodigious.*

Not only had the great miracle announced taken place at the time and place mentioned by the children: it had been on a scale of magnificence beyond all expectation! *The reality of the apparitions had been demonstrated.*

From this solemn moment Cova da Iria was considered by the people as a holy place, a real sanctuary, and a new Lourdes to which a stream of pilgrims, strong and infirm, continued to flow without intermission. Far from encouraging these manifestations, the clergy continued to hold itself apart. But Our Lady of the Rosary was pleased to encourage strongly the devotion of her pilgrims to Fatima. Not only did she grant many cures but she even aroused their enthusiasm by renewing on certain days a most touching prodigy. It is known that the Rosary devotion gets its name from rosarium, "a crown of roses," because the *Hail Marys* recited are considered as so many mystic roses which the faithful throw to their heavenly Mother. Now while the pilgrims recited the Rosary, thus throwing to their heavenly Mother the mystical flowers of the *Hail Mary*, Our Lady of the Rosary of Fatima was pleased to respond maternally to their filial devotion by causing to fall on them from time to time *a veritable shower of flowers and*

[1] A brief notice had indeed announced abroad that a solar phenomenon had just taken place in Portugal. But this laconic information passed unperceived by people who had not followed the events at Fatima, and whose major preoccupation was the war. Besides, the clergy preserved always great reserve about Fatima, and did not seek in any way to spread the news.

rose petals! One can easily imagine how these extraordinary manifestations of the tenderness of the maternal Heart of Mary went straight to the hearts of her children, and fed the sacred flame of an ardent love for their good Mother of Fatima!

On week-days pilgrims came alone or in small groups. On Sundays the number increased. On the thirteenth of each month, and especially in May (the anniversary of the first apparition) and in October (the anniversary of the Great Prodigy), they came in tens of thousands to Cova da Iria to recite the Rosary, to ask for graces needed, and to give thanks for favours received.

Before July 13th, 1917, the faithful had already raised a rustic wooden arch above the little tree of the apparitions. On April 28th, 1919, they replaced the primitive arch by a little stone chapel, called the *Chapel of the Apparitions,* built beside the tree with the alms the pilgrims left there.

The pilgrimage and cult of Our Lady of the Rosary of Fatima thus continued to grow with an irresistible force; but it was left completely to the devotion of the faithful, without the intervention of any official religious organisation.

CHAPTER II

The Attack of the Secular Authorities

THE solar prodigy of Fatima, attested by seventy thousand witnesses, and even by the impious Avelino d'Almeida in his celebrated article in the big Lisbon newspaper, *O Seculo,* was a really stunning blow to the Free-thinkers of the country. They were so stupefied that for more than a week not one of them dared raise his voice! But as soon as the first impressions began to wear away, they launched a violent campaign against what they called "the growing superstition of Fatima". The details of these attacks make interesting reading in the books recommended, but we shall give here only a few of them.

On the night of the 23rd–24th October, 1917, a band of Carbonari, with the complicity of the civil authority, organised at Santarem, the administrative centre of the prefecture on which Fatima depends, a parody of a procession in which were exhibited objects stolen secretly from Cova da Iria. The big Lisbon newspapers deplored these vulgar proceedings; the Catholics, who no longer allowed themselves to be intimidated, lodged a lively protest with the local administration and with the Ministry of the Interior.

Towards the end of the month, the anticlericals spread through the whole country a manifesto addressed "To the Portuguese Free-thinkers." We give a few extracts: ". . . Fatima is a shameful comedy, a reactionary manifestation, an attempt at mass-suggestion! . . . Now a miracle announced in advance has been invented and that in the twentieth century! . . . Citizens! An attempt is being made to drag the Portuguese people back to the Middle Ages, to dehumanise and brutalise them! . . . It is for us who are instructed to show the people the stupidity of the supernatural! The laws of nature are unchangeable and these are no miracles! . . ."

The Catholics proudly exposed the illogicality of this hollow nonsensical verbiage, which instead of denying the events of Fatima or trying to give a natural explanation, restricted itself to being cynical and insulting, *thus showing clearly that there was not a serious argument to oppose to these resounding*

99

facts! This manifesto was the cry of despair of the sectarianism then in power, which was beginning to feel its head crushed under the victorious heel of the heavenly apparition of Fatima! The struggle had now definitely started. It would last several years with varying fortunes. The short-lived Government of the patriot Sidonio Pais, who took office on December 7th, 1917, was only a passing respite for Portuguese Catholics. He restored order to the country, recalled from exile the Bishop of Porto, and Cardinal Belo, the Patriarch of Lisbon; modified some laws hostile to the Catholic religion, and gave hope of raising up the country from its ruins. But Sidonio Pais was assassinated by the Carbonari on December 14th, 1918, and his work of reconstruction fell with him.

From December, 1918, to 1920, the Pastors and Mayors of the region of Fatima once more received repeated and menacing commands to prevent pilgrims from going to Cova da Iria. On May 13th, 1920, the anniversary of the first apparition, the Prefect compelled the Mayors to stop all vehicles going towards Fatima, and surrounded the place of the apparitions with several regiments of the Republican Guard. But the witnesses of the Solar Prodigy of 1917 had too lively a faith to allow themselves to be frightened off by human prohibitions. With tenacious obstinacy they overcame all impediments! On the closed routes they descended from their vehicles and continued on foot; while around Cova da Iria, the growing crowd quickly broke the cordon of soldiers who, themselves out of sympathy with the odious task imposed on them, readily declared themselves unable to keep back these waves of humanity. Finally, even soldiers were seen to go and pray with the pilgrims before the little "Chapel of the Apparitions."

But the intolerant zeal of the sectarians did not cease. The pious pilgrims of Fatima continued to be constantly annoyed by repeated prohibitions, fines and arrests.

On the night of March 6th, 1922, *the little Chapel raised up by the piety of the faithful was blown up with dynamite.* A curious fact, which the people attributed to the protection of heaven, is that all the bombs exploded, except the one that was to blow up the remains of the tree of the apparitions! The news of this odious attempt caused a wave of indignation throughout the country, and protests from the Catholics made themselves heard even in Parliament. Without venturing to approve openly of the attempt, the Government threatened, however, to employ severe measures to put a stop to the "reactionary movement of Fatima."

In answer to these threats, the faithful launched the idea of a pilgrimage of reparation. On October 13th, 1922, ten thousand pilgrims went from the Church of Fatima in a procession of reparation to Cova da Iria, a distance of two miles, where they assisted at Mass celebrated in the open air. This local reparation was followed, on May 13th, 1923, by a pilgrimage of national reparation, in which over sixty thousand persons from all classes of society, and all provinces in the country, took part. The offerings on this day were so plentiful that the required sum was soon collected to build a chapel more beautiful still than the first. The Prefect of Santarem wished at all cost to prevent this pilgrimage, which he called "a parade of all the reactionary forces in the country"; but the sub-Prefect of Ourem judged it more prudent not to execute the orders received for fear of being submerged.

Gradually the peaceful but resolute strength of this multitude, which confessed its faith so loudly, ended by triumphing over the sectarianism of the Government and its functionaries, who no longer dared insist!

On May 13th, 1924, Our Lady of the Rosary of Fatima rewarded once more the love of her pilgrims, by showering down on them from heaven a magnificent rain of flowers. Thenceforth the pilgrims of Fatima continued to come with all freedom, increasing in numbers and in fervour.

CHAPTER III

The Ecclesiastical Authority

Attitude of Prudent Reserve

IN 1917, the parish of Fatima belonged to the diocese of Lisbon. From the beginning of the apparitions, His Eminence the Cardinal Patriarch had forbidden the clergy of the diocese to take the least part in these events, as yet so ill-defined. It was simply a measure of prudence, before the question had been examined. This episcopal prohibition was so strictly observed, that the good Pastors of Fatima and the neighbourhood were finally eyed with disfavour by the faithful, who accused them of making common cause with the enemies of the Church.

But the Great Prodigy of October 13th, 1917, had completely changed the situation. The mass of the people no longer doubted the divine origin of these apparitions; and the pilgrimages and cult of Our Lady of the Rosary of Fatima were assuming such proportions, that it became urgently necessary for the ecclesiastical authority to take up a definite position in face of events of such a serious nature. As early as October 15th, 1917, the Pastor of Fatima sent a report to the patriarchal Curia asking what line of conduct he should follow. The reply, dated November 3rd, prescribed a serious enquiry into the facts.

The New Bishop of Leiria

By a brief of January 17th, 1918, Pope Benedict XV, doubtless as a result of these weighty events, re-established the ancient diocese of Leiria, and incorporated in it the parish of Fatima. Then on Saturday, May 15th, 1920, he appointed as Bishop of the new diocese the Professor of Theology of the Seminary of Porto, Dr. Jose Alves Correia da Silva, who was consecrated on July 25th, and took possession of his diocese on August 5th, 1920.

The new Bishop of Leiria-Fatima took cognizance of the

reports sent by the Pastor of Fatima and by the Dean of Porto-de-Moz, but in spite of the most pressing requests to make a statement, he persistently observed a wise reserve while awaiting the development of the situation.

However, as he gradually saw that the finger of God was manifesting itself more clearly in the events of Fatima, His Lordship decided to adopt several provisionary measures, while reserving definitive judgment on the whole case for a later date. Thus, in October, 1921, he gave permission for a Low Mass at the site of the apparitions on days when large numbers were present. At the same time he decided to purchase, as a measure of prudence, a large area of land which the people willingly sold him.

CHAPTER IV

The Canonical Process and Ecclesiastical Approbation

On May 3rd, 1922, His Lordship the Bishop of Leiria published the decree opening the "canonical process" or official ecclesiastical enquiry into the events of Fatima. This canonical Commission, composed of seven members noted for their learning and virtue, made its final report, the result of long years of work, on April 14th, 1929. After spending many months more in a detailed study of this document of thirty-one chapters and in preparing his decision, His Lordship Dom Jose Correia de Silva finally published his "Pastoral Letter on the Cult of Our Lady of the Rosary of Fatima." After briefly exposing the facts as well as the reasons for his decision, he concluded: "We judge it well:

1. "To declare worthy of credence the visions with which the children were favoured at Cova da Iria, in the Parish of Fatima, diocese of Leiria, on the 13th of each month from May to October, 1917.
2. "To authorise officially the cult of Our Lady of Fatima."

This remarkable document, awaited such a long time, was read and promulgated at Cova da Iria itself, during a pilgrimage on October 13th, 1930, before a crowd of over 100,000 pilgrims.

This official ecclesiastical approbation produced through the whole country a rapturous joy. Immediately the idea of a national pilgrimage of thanksgiving was launched, which took place on May 13th, 1931. It comprised over 300,000 pilgrims, an incalculable number of priests and all the Portuguese Bishops, His Eminence Cardinal Cerejeira, Patriarch of Lisbon, who presided officially over the pilgrimage, explained to the crowd that all the Bishops of the country had gathered here to thank Our Lady of the Rosary for the visit she had deigned to pay to Portugal, and to ask her to preserve the country from the wicked atheistic movement.

Then all the Bishops together solemnly consecrated Portugal to the Immaculate Heart of Mary.

In 1936 the Portuguese Bishops made a vow to go, all together to Fatima to renew there this consecration to the Immaculate Heart of Mary, if the Blessed Virgin would deign to preserve their country from the Communist revolution which was raging in adjoining Spain. Their prayer having been granted in spite of the numerous attempts of the "Reds," the "Great Pilgrimage of the anti-Communist Vow" took place on May 13th, 1938. It brought to Fatima 500,000 of the faithful, more than 100 priests and 20 prelates who solemnly renewed the consecration of their country to the Immaculate Heart of Mary. Simultaneously, all the parishes and churches of Portugal rendered to their heavenly Liberator, the same homage of love, gratitude and fidelity.

CHAPTER V

Fatima in the Eternal City

WE now come to the effect produced by all these events at Fatima *in ecclesiastical circles in Rome,* always extremely reserved in matters of this kind.

In reply to a report of the Portuguese Bishops, Benedict XV wrote on April 29th, 1918, that he had always hoped that the depressing situation of the Church in Portugal was only passing, because the ardent devotion of that country to the Immaculate Conception *merited for it an extraordinary aid from the Mother of God.*[1] It is beyond doubt that these grave words of the Holy Father alluded to the great events of Fatima, which were then occupying all minds in Portugal.

On November 1st, 1926, *the Apostolic Nuncio* at Lisbon came spontaneously to Fatima, where, after praying and addressing the people, he granted a partial indulgence.

On January 21st, 1927, *the Sacred Congregation of Rites* granted to the Sanctuary of Fatima the indult of the Mass of Our Lady of the Rosary.

On May 13th, 1928, the first stone of the Basilica of Fatima was blessed in the presence of a crowd of 300,000 pilgrims. A description of this great pilgrimage, published in the *Osservatore Romano* on June 13th, 1928, was the subject of much comment.

More significant still is *the personal act of Pope Pius XI,* who, on January 9th, 1929, at an audience of the Portuguese Seminary in Rome, was pleased to offer to each seminarist two pictures of Our Lady of Fatima. On December 6th of the same year, Pius XI wished to bless personally at the Vatican the statue of Our Lady of Fatima, sent from Portugal for the Portuguese Seminary in Rome. Short of giving a definitive judgment, the Sovereign Pontiff could not have manifested in a more expressive manner his opinion and his good will towards these events of Fatima. It is also known that Pius XI wished to read all the acts of the Canonical

---

[1] Acta Apostolicae Sedis, 1918, p. 230: "Hane spem confirmabat flagrans erga Virginem Immaculatam pietas . . . quae quidem pietas singulare quoddam divinae auxilium merebatur."

Process of Fatima in order to acquaint himself personally with such an extraordinary marvel.

On May 13th, 1930, the Portuguese Seminary in Rome celebrated the anniversary of the first apparition of Fatima, and the *Sacred Congregation of Rites* granted it the indult of celebrating the Mass of Our Lady of the Rosary under the rite of a double of the first class.

On October 1st, 1930, the *Sacred Penitentiary* granted to the faithful who visit individually the Sanctuary of Fatima and pray for the Pope's intentions, a partial indulgence; and to those who make the pilgrimage in a group, a plenary indulgence once a month. As has been said above, it was on October 13th of that year that His Lordship the Bishop of Leiria was to promulgate his Pastoral Letter approving officially the apparitions and cult of Our Lady of Fatima; and it will be observed that these indulgences granted at Rome on October 1st came just in time to prepare minds to receive with entire confidence the proximate episcopal approbation, *which the Holy See has thus discreetly supported*.

The Apostolic Nuncio at Lisbon took part in the great pilgrimage to Fatima on May 13th, 1931; and the following year presided over the pilgrimage of May 13th.

Furthermore, on November 10th, 1933, Pius XI, in recommending Catholic Action to the Portuguese Bishops, wrote: "In your country so flourishing with the Christian spirit . . . *which quite recently the Virgin Mother of God has designed to favour with extraordinary benefits,* it will not be difficult to find good citizens, who will spontaneously and willingly give their names to this militia of Jesus Christ"—really remarkable words which caused a great stir in Portugal.

Pius XII, in his Apostolic Letter "Saeculo exeunte octavo," of June 13th, 1940, addressed to the Bishops of Portugal to develop the Portuguese missions, said also: ". . . *Let the faithful, when reciting the Rosary so strongly recommended by Our Lady of Fatima, not omit to address an invocation to the Blessed Virgin in favour of missionary vocations.*" And at the end of the letter: "God will then bless this holy crusade (of the Missions) and the chivalrous Portuguese people, *under the auspices of Our Lady of the Rosary of Fatima, the Blessed Virgin of the Rosary, who obtained the victory of Lepanto*".

In their collective Pastoral Letter of 1942, the Portuguese Bishops wrote on this subject: "We are happy to see *the Supreme Authority of the Vicar of Jesus Christ evoke thus the testimony of Fatima* and proclaim Urbi et orbi the name of Our Lady of Fatima in an Apostolic Letter addressed to the Portuguese Bishops, but published for the whole world."

On erecting in Mozambique, in 1941, *the new diocese* of Nampula, the Holy See gave it officially as Patroness Our Lady of Fatima (A.A.S. 33 (1941), 16).

On the occasion of the celebration of the 25th Anniversary of Fatima, *The Osservatore Romano* of Sunday, May 10th, 1942, published eight large columns in folio with illustrations, on the apparitions of Our Lady of Fatima.

On May 13th, 1942, was issued, also from the Vatican Press, the 4th edition of Fr. Fonseca's book: *Le Meraviglie di Fatima,* with the *Imprimatur of the Vicar-General of Vatican City.*

On October 31st, 1942, *His Holiness Pius XII* associated himself with the closing celebrations of the Jubilee of Fatima; and in his radio message to the Portuguese nation, made the consecration of the world, and of Russia in particular, to the Immaculate Heart of Mary.

Again, on May 13th, 1946, the Sovereign Pontiff was pleased to send a Legate *a latere* to crown in his (the Pope's) name the statue of Our Lady of Fatima in the midst of great rejoicings. But what stands out as perhaps the most significant gesture of the late Pope is that he should have decreed that the solemn official closing of the 1950 Jubilee Year should take place at Fatima. As in 1946, he sent a special legate to represent him, while the Holy Father himself spoke to the assembled multitudes over the radio. The crowd, made up of pilgrims from all parts of the world, was estimated at one million.

Quite true, neither the apparitions nor the message of Fatima are articles of Faith, and the infallibility of the Church is not involved in any of the acts we have just recounted. But without any definitive judgment, the Holy See could not have manifested in a more expressive manner its opinion and good-will towards the events of Fatima.

CHAPTER VI

What Became of the Seers of Fatima

THE lives of the three children of Fatima were entirely transformed by the heavenly apparitions. While fulfilling the duties of their state with the greatest fidelity, those children seemed now to live only on Rosaries and sacrifices, which they offered in a spirit of reparation to obtain peace and the conversion of sinners. They deprived themselves of water during the periods of great heat; they gave their lunch to poor children; they bore about their loins a thick cord that even drew blood; they abstained from little innocent pleasures and urged one another to the practice of prayer and penance with an ardour comparable to that of the great saints.

Francis was struck down by the well-known Spanish influenza in December, 1918. The little patient suffered for several months always devout, and very faithful to his Rosary which he recited eight or nine times a day. When he no longer had the strength to pronounce the words he said them mentally. On Thursday, April 3rd, 1919, he made his First Communion on his death-bed, all radiant with happiness. On the following day, Friday, April 4th, at 10 o'clock in the evening, he died the death of the elect, with a smile on his lips. He was ten years and nine months old.

Jacinta was attacked also by the Spanish influenza almost at the same time as her brother Francis. She too spoke of nothing else than of reciting the Rosary and offering sacrifices for sinners. One day she confided to Lucy: "The Blessed Virgin has told me that I shall go to a hospital in Lisbon, that I shall not see my parents again, that after suffering much I shall die all alone, but that I must not be afraid, for she will come and take me to heaven."

Indeed, towards the end of January, 1920, she was taken to Lisbon to be operated upon for a purulent pleurisy. There she immediately impressed all by her candour, her modesty, her great patience, her perfect submission, her continued prayer and ardent love for Holy Communion which she received every day except when prevented by illness. The Blessed Virgin continued to encourage this heroic virtue by

109

her apparitions. One day, when the Superioress came to see her, Jacinta asked her quite naturally: "Could you come back a little later? I am expecting the Blessed Virgin any minute!" And, all transfigured the child looked fixedly at a definite spot. On another occasion she was heard to say "That place must be left free, for that is where the Blessed Virgin stood."

The effects of these visits from heaven manifested themselves not only in the supernatural wisdom of the child's words, but also in her predictions. One of the doctors who attended her in Lisbon asked her to recommend him to the Blessed Virgin when she went to heaven. Jacinta promised to do so; and then looking at the doctor she said to him: "You will follow me soon!" To another doctor, who recommended himself and his daughter to her prayers, she promised to pray for them and added: "You will follow me soon; first your daughter and then yourself!" These predictions, as well as several others, were fulfilled to the letter.

On Friday, February 20th, 1920, Jacinta asked for the last Sacraments saying that she was going to die. The Pastor came and heard her confession at 8 o'clock in the evening. She insisted on receiving the holy Viaticum, assuring them that she was going to die. They answered that she would receive it on the following morning because there was no hurry. The child submitted, but at about 10 o'clock in the morning expired peacefully, attended only by her nurse. She was hardly ten years old.

At the news of her death people came from everywhere to see *"the little angel."* Their enthusiasm naturally increased when it was perceived that the body of "the little angel" *exhaled a delicious perfume of flowers.* The body had to be left exposed for three days to satisfy the devotion of the people!

Placed then in a leaden coffin, filled with quicklime, Jacinta's body was taken to Ourem, near Fatima, where the Barons of Alvaizere obtained, as a favour, permission to keep it in their family vault.

Finally, on September 13th, 1935, His Lordship the Bishop of Leiria had the body of the little seer transported to the cemetery of Fatima where it was laid with the mortal remains of her brother Francis, in a pretty marble vault made expressly for that purpose. *The work preparatory to the introduction of her cause of canonisation has begun.*

Lucy is the only one of the three seers of Fatima who is

still alive. For some years she was seen often at Cova da Iria, modest and pious, reciting the Rosary with the crowd. In 1921 she entered the Orphanage of the Dorothean Sisters at Porto. In 1925 she sought admission as a lay-sister in that Society, and in 1928 *made her religious profession* with the name of Sister Mary-Lucy of Sorrows.

The blessed Virgin continues to favour her with her visits, but for the moment nothing is made public. For some years she was living in a community near Porto (Portugal), always industrious, intelligent, pious, but above all well hidden, and entirely outside the magnificent religious movement of Fatima that the Blessed Virgin started with her as intermediary. On May 20th and 21st, 1946, Sister Lucy came back to Fatima for the first time since her departure in 1921. She was accompanied by her Superior and by His Lordship, the Bishop. They travelled incognito.

On Holy Thursday, March 25th, 1948, Sister Lucy entered the Carmel of Coimbra, Portugal. She made her religious profession, taking the name of Sister Lucy of the Immaculate Heart on May 31st, Feast of Mary, Mediatrix of All Graces. She knows that the cult of Our Lady of the Rosary of Fatima has assumed immense proportions, and that is enough for her happiness.

The memoirs and depositions of Lucy have, naturally enough, been of capital importance in throwing light on the tremendous drama that took place in the Cova da Iria in 1917.

She emerged from her Cloister and stood at the Pope's side during his visit to the Shrine of Fatima for the Golden Jubilee celebrations in 1967. But she is rarely seen nowadays and no statements by her have been made public in recent years.

She is seen occasionally by Father Luis Kondor S.V.D., Postulator for the Causes of the two younger seers, Francisco and Jacinta. She has seen her prophecies concerning the spread of error from Russia fulfilled in a remarkable way. And Our Lady has indeed used her to spread devotion to the Immaculate Heart for this is also being brought about by the great world movement in which she has played so important a part.

CHAPTER VII

Appeal to Priests

DEAR Brothers in Our Lord, knowing that our holy Faith, founded on the revelation and miracles of Our Lord and the Apostles has no need of being proved by new miracles, you are inclined as a matter of principle not to attribute too much importance to apparitions and present-day prodigies however authentic they may be. Nevertheless, events as extraordinary as those of Fatima merit in a special way your attention, above all since the Pope has consecrated the world to the Immaculate Heart of Mary. The Blessed Virgin, who has not disdained to come down from heaven and bring her message, accompanying it by such a great profusion of miracles and a love still greater, certainly desires her priests to work for the diffusion of this message of salvation. The souls entrusted to your care ought not to be deprived of the effects of faith and love that the message of Fatima can produce in them.

Try therefore to give a few sermons or instructions on the events of Fatima. Re-awaken the faith of your people by the authentic account of prodigies so recent and unique in history! Show them also the great esteem of the Saints and the Popes for the devotion of the Rosary, which we neglect so much. Point out clearly how the Blessed Virgin herself, already at Lourdes, but more directly still at Fatima, has come to confirm their teaching. She has presented the Rosary to the world as a means, simple in truth, but divinely chosen, and still efficacious in our days, of regenerating souls, families, parishes and society itself that is in urgent need of such a renewal.

In recommending the Rosary, priests are only following the exhortations and personal example of the great Popes: Leo XIII and Pius XI.

Mgr. Touchet, Bishop of Orleans, loved to relate how he had surprised Leo XIII "in the very act of reciting his Rosary some months before his death". Having gone afterwards to Cardinal Rampolla he ventured to say: "He prays very much to the Blessed Virgin, this great diplomat!" "Ah!" replied the Cardinal, "you have seen his Rosary hanging on his chair? Well, you may be sure that he was reciting it before you went

112

in, and that he took it up again after your departure. When he is not working he recites his Rosary".

The same Pope Leo XIII in inscribing his name in the Association of the Perpetual Rosary said: "I choose the hour of ten to eleven in the evening on the first day of the month, because that is the time I say the Rosary each evening in my Chapel!" He recited it in company with his nephew Count Ricardo, and with such piety that he seemed to relish each *Hail Mary* as if he recited it for the first time in his life!

Pius XI said to Mgr. Richaud, Auxiliary Bishop of Versailles: "Tell your priests to pray very much! Tell them that the Pope recites his Rosary every day; that as long as the Pope has not recited his Rosary, the Pope's day is not over!" and in another audience, he added familiarly: "Yesterday it was already late, we were very tired, and we still had our third Rosary to say".

And if the Pope, with the charge of the Universal Church, finds ways of saying his entire Rosary every day, what excuse would we have before God for not reciting at least one Rosary, when the world has such need of it and Our Lady of Fatima has asked it of us!

Let us then preach Our Lady of the Rosary of Fatima. Let us get people to recite the Rosary with its traditional mysteries, adding the short prayer given by Our Lady of Fatima: "O my Jesus, forgive us our sins, save us from the fire of hell, lead all souls to heaven, and help especially those who most need Your mercy".

Let us propagate the devotion of the First Saturdays and let us not forget consecration to the Immaculate Heart of Mary. Let us consecrate to her our parish, and ask other groups, parochial works, various categories of persons and families, to make the same consecration.

Many priests have already made known to their flocks the heavenly Message of Fatima, and have always aroused a real enthusiasm. Try loyally in your turn. Preach on Fatima; spread literature amongst your people. You will see that Our Lady of Fatima will not fail to reward your confidence!

CHAPTER VIII

Appeal to the Faithful

CHRISTIAN SOUL, you have just read the great wonders of Our Lady of the Rosary of Fatima, and are still gripped by them. *Do not keep this booklet to yourself,* but get those about you to read it and make it known as much as possible. Become the apostle of Fatima, and our heavenly Mother will bless you.

Remember also that the reading of this book is a grace obtained for you by the Blessed Virgin, to which you must correspond by welcoming her heavenly message and putting it faithfully into practice. In circumstances similar to the ones in which we live, Our Lady of Fatima has come down from heaven to ask us "to recite the Rosary to obtain the end of the war through her intercession, because only she can come to our aid!" In the message of October 13th, she asked again for the recitation of the Rosary, amendment of life and penance. And it is to help us also to believe in her word and to obey her demands that Our Lady of Fatima has deigned to work the wonderful Solar Prodigy. Let us not harden our hearts, but let us give to our heavenly Mother what she asks of us in our interests. Let us make a good Confession and fervent Communion. Then let us begin a truly Christian life, faithful to the Commandments of God and the Church, as well as to the duties of our state in life. Finally, let us, with firm decision, fix for ourselves a time in the day for reciting our Rosary. Let us not listen to the false excuses of the devil, our imagination, and our daily habits, which strive to convince us that it is impossible! The times in which we live are not ordinary; neither let our conduct be ordinary. Let us not hesitate to change our habits resolutely, if that is necessary, and let us not wait until severe trials come and make us change them perforce! If Pius XI himself, in spite of his heavy charge, never went to bed without reciting the whole Rosary (*i.e.,* fifteen Mysteries) with his household, who will dare say that he has not the time to recite everyday, at least one Rosary, in order to obtain from God, through the intercession of the Blessed Virgin, the removal of all the scourges which chastise the world?

Let us then resolutely promise Our Heavenly Mother to recite our Rosary daily, if possible with the family. A mother whose children recite the Rosary daily can die in peace; she is sure of meeting them all again in heaven one day.[1] In order to please our Heavenly Mother let us try to add the two other Rosaries which we can say when working or on the road, when coming or going, or even in bed at night.

Let us hasten also *to make to the Immaculate Heart of Mary the Consecration* of our person, our family and of the works of which we have the charge or the responsibility.

Let us clearly understand the gravity of the events that are taking place at present, and of those that will inevitably follow if. . . ! Let us pray with all our hearts, and let our prayer be sincere accompanied by a true conversion, by a radical amendment of life. *This is the least that is demanded of all Christians.*

As for those faithful souls who understand better the love of God, and the exceptional gravity of the trials through which we are passing, *they must go still further.* Let them seek to answer the various appeals of Our Lady of Fatima, as if they had been addressed to them personally. "Do you wish to offer yourselves to God to bear all the sufferings it will please Him to send you, in reparation for the sins which offend Him, and for the conversion of sinners?" "Sacrifice yourselves for sinners! and say often: "Oh Jesus it is for love of You, for the conversion of sinners, and in reparation for the offences committed against the Immaculate Heart of Mary!"—"Pray, pray very much, and make many sacrifices for sinners! Remember that many souls go to hell, because there is no one to pray and make sacrifices for them!"

"Poor Blessed Virgin", said Jacinta on her deathbed, "I pity her so much, so much!"—let us then give the Immaculate Heart of our Heavenly Mother the great joy of seeing her message heeded, and faithfully put into practice. If we do this we shall draw the blessing of God on ourselves, on our family, and on our country.

---

[1] "No matter how criminal a sinner may be, if he perseveres in his devotion to Mary, he will be saved." (St. Hilary).

"He who trusts in Me through the Rosary will not perish." (Promise of the Most Blessed Virgin Mary to Blessed Alain de la Roche).

CHAPTER IX

The 25th Anniversary and the Solemn Crowning of Our Lady of Fatima

In 1942, on the occasion of the celebration of the 25th anniversary of the apparitions of Our Lady of the Rosary at Fatima and the Great Solar Prodigy, *the Portuguese Bishops published a collective Pastoral Letter*. Here are the main points:

Our very dear brothers, despite the sorrowful nature of the times, we invite you to rejoice with a holy joy because the Lord is nigh, since He has sent us His Holy Mother. You are not ignorant of that great event. It was in 1917. "Portugal, exhausted internally by a wicked religious persecution, and externally by a bloody war, seemed to be on the verge of extinction, only waiting for the stone to fall and cover forever, the discredited remains of a people that had once been great.

"It was then that the Blessed Virgin appeared at Fatima infusing a new spirit into the souls of the Portuguese people and spreading over the country the rays of her re-invigorating light. Clearly the finger of God was there! *If someone, who had closed his eyes 25 years ago, were to open them now, he would no longer recognise Portugal, so profound and extensive is the transformation effected by that modest and unnoticed factor—the apparitions of Fatima.* Truly the Blessed Virgin wishes to save Portugal!"

One thing is necessary, we must will to save ourselves by obeying her. We must therefore welcome with all our souls the heavenly message of Fatima, declare an implacable war on sin under all its forms, repent of our faults, and do penance . . .

A second reason for rejoicing and giving thanks to God is that *the Sovereign Pontiff, Pius XII, was consecrated Bishop on Sunday, May 13th, 1917, at the very moment of the first apparition of our Lady of Fatima.* Is not this coincidence symbolic? . . .

Finally, the Bishops arranged the magnificent programme of celebrations. In each parish of the country: a Mission, general ringing of bells, meetings of Confraternities, solemn offices with General Communion, Exposition of the Blessed Sacrament, processions, etc.: two great national Congresses, one for the young men at Fatima, another for the young women at Lisbon, at which the miraculous statue of Our Lady of Fatima would be borne in triumph; foundation of *leagues of Christian modesty,* in which everyone would engage to ban entirely all unbecoming fashions and indecent cinemas, etc.

Thus, despite the sorrowful nature of the times, Portugal has celebrated in a noteworthy fashion the 25th anniversary of the apparitions and incomparable prodigies of Our Lady of Fatima!

It was at the closing of these Jubilee Celebrations, on October 31st, 1942, that His Holiness Pius XII consecrated the world to the Immaculate Heart of Mary, as Our Lady of Fatima had requested.

The Crowning

On the occasion of the Jubilee of the apparitions, the women of Portugal had offered their wedding rings and jewellery to make a Crown for Our Lady of Fatima, Queen of Portugal. The Bishops decided to postpone this Crowning until the National Pilgrimage after the war, when the entire nation went once more to thank its heavenly Queen and patron for having preserved it again from the horrors of the worldwide war. This magnificent ceremony of the Crowning took place on May 13th, 1946. Pope Pius XII was graciously pleased to associate himself with it and sent his Legate *a latere,* Cardinal Aloysius Masella, to crown in his (the Pope's) name *Our Lady of Fatima as Queen of Portugal and Queen of the World*—Regina Mundi.

The attendance was most impressive: 800,000 faithful, the whole of the Portuguese Episcopacy, numberless clergy, the army and heads of State. The President of the League of Catholic Women hands the magnificent golden crown to the representative of the head of the State. The latter passes it on to the Cardinal Legate, representing the Vicar of Jesus Christ, who places it on the forehead of Our Lady of Fatima. The applause and hosannas were blended with tears of devotion, of love and gratitude of all the people who acclaim Mary as Queen and Jesus Christ as King. The consecration of Portugal to the Immaculate Heart of Mary is renewed; then the loud-speakers enable us to hear the voice of the Sovereign Pontiff: "Your presence at this Sanctuary in incalculable numbers proves that the Immaculate Queen, whose Immaculate and Compassionate Heart has produced the miracle of Fatima, has granted more than fully our prayers (to preserve you from the horrors of war). Think of these last thirty years, the crises gone through, the benefits received! How can we return thanks worthily?" Then Pope Pius XII explains that Mary "by Jesus, with Jesus and depending on Jesus, is Queen—Queen by grace, by divine relationship, by winning of favours and by choice; Queen of a realm as large as that of her Son—God, since nothing is exempt from His domain. But her royalty is essentially that of a mother and wholly gracious".

"Fatima is a fount of graces, wonders and miracles which flow down in torrents on Portugal, and thence spread throughout the whole Church and the entire world. Cova da Iria is the blessed oasis, saturated with the supernatural, where one experiences more fully, the all-embracing patronage of Our Lady of Fatima, where all feel nearer to her Immaculate Heart with its pulsation of an immense tenderness and a maternal anxiety for you and the whole world. . ." "Yes, crown her not only Queen of Portugal but Queen of Peace and Queen of the World because she helps it to find peace again and to rise again from its ruins. But while crowning her, you thereby enrol yourselves in the sacred crusade for the conquest or the re-conquest of her realm which is that of God and you undertake to work to make her loved, venerated and served in the family, in society and throughout the world!" (Acta Apos. Sedis, 1946, p. 164).

CHAPTER X

Pilgrim Virgin

The National Tour

THE sanctuary of Fatima has become the religious centre of Portugal, and every year, one Portuguese in six goes there to renew his supernatural life. But how many invalids, children, old people, mothers of families, etc., are not able to leave their homes to go to Fatima? In 1942, at the request of the faithful the statue of Our Lady of Fatima was brought to Lisbon for a Catholic Youth Congress. This first voyage was in truth a triumph, and resulted in such wonderful faith, frequentation of the Sacraments and lasting conversions, that it was renewed in 1946 after the ceremony of the "Crowning". It was during the course of this second journey that the touching "Miracle of the Doves" happened, which aroused the general enthusiasm of the people and the Press. A person had brought white doves which she let loose during the passing of the procession of Our Lady of Fatima. Having circled around in the air, the doves came to rest at the feet of the statue. Regardless of the shouts of the crowd and the noise of the band, they accompanied the statue to Lisbon, entered the church with it and remained there during all the ceremonies, day and night. Then, faithfully following our Lady of Fatima on the boat which crossed over the Tagus, the doves returned with it to the Shrine of Fatima where they eventually settled down. Everyone thought this miraculous as it was so extraordinary and so touching. But this admiration grew much greater throughout the whole country, when people learned through articles in the newspapers that a similar marvel had taken place at Rio de Janeiro (Brazil) at the moment when, uniting with Portugal, the grand ceremonies in honour of Our Lady of Fatima were being held. Since then Our Lady of Fatima occasionally leaves her shrine at Fatima to make a tour of different dioceses and parishes in Portugal which lovingly compete to receive her worthily and on which she heaps her spiritual and temporal blessings.

In December, 1947, Our Lady of Fatima set out again to

travel through the two provinces of Alenteigo and Algarve, in the South of Portugal, and was received everywhere with the greatest enthusiasm. And once again while passing through Beja, about sixty miles from Fatima, the touching "Miracle of the Doves" was repeated. On January 12th, 1948, the statue returned in haste to Fatima for the traditional pilgrimage of the 13th, accompanied by three Bishops and a concourse of the faithful from the two provinces visited. The five doves of Beja were always at their post, at the feet of the Blessed Virgin, and drew from all who assisted tears of tenderness and devotion.

The European Tour

The message of Fatima is universal; it is directed to the whole world. When crowning Our Lady of Fatima on May 13th, 1946, Pope Pius XII expressly declared in his radio message that he intended to crown her "Queen of Peace and Queen of the World" to help the world to recover peace and to rise from its ruins. In conformity with these views and sentiments, several of the clergy of countries ravaged by war requested that Our Lady of Fatima be borne solemnly through all the frontiers of Europe up to the boundaries of Poland, that she might invite all Christian peoples to unite in brotherhood under her auspices and bring to them, with her heavenly message, consoling promises of a sincere and lasting peace.

The pious and worthy proposal was communicated to Sister Lucy who rapturously exclaimed: "But why stop at Poland? We must go to Russia. I am going to pray that Our Lady of Fatima can gain entrance into Russia."[1] And for this "European Tour" Sister Lucy expressed the wish to choose herself a statue made in accordance with her own directions.

On May 13th, 1947, this statue was blessed and started on its way to make a tour of Europe as circumstances permitted.

The journey through Spain was a real triumph. Here are the actual words of a Spanish Bishop on the visit of the Pilgrim Virgin to his diocese:

"In all small parishes and working-class colonies an average

[1] A Pilgrim Statue was indeed taken to Moscow and reposes in the U.S. Embassy there.

of 95–97 per cent received the Sacraments. The average for the whole diocese was 90 per cent . . .

"The visit of the Blessed Virgin of Fatima to our Diocese has been in truth a Mission in the truest sense of the word, and has borne fruits of sanctification more abundantly than the best organised Mission heretofore. It has been a Diocesan Mission the results of which would be difficult to exceed . . .

"A Missionary Son of the Immaculate Heart of Mary told us a few days after the beginning of the pilgrimage: 'We do not need any more Missionaries. The Blessed Virgin by her presence alone achieves more than us all with our preaching and labours.'

"This supernatural fruit, the achievement of the pilgrimage, claimed the attention of all and provoked intense discussion. Priests in particular were surprised and astonished. We saw many of them overcome with emotion to the point of tears. Their verdict was: *'This is a great miracle of Our Lady.'* " (Vicente, Bishop of Solsona. Reprinted from the *Voice of Fatima*, August, 1951).

The people, invited and led by their Bishops and clergy, came in procession to greet the heavenly Messenger of Fatima who deigned to reward the faith and love of her children whilst scattering before them genuine miracles.

At the French-Spanish border, the passage of Our Lady of Fatima produced already its first effect in the fraternisation of the races. The Spanish procession took place on June 18th, 1947, led by Mgr. Vallester, Bishop of Vitoria. The French procession, precided over by Mgr. Terrier, Bishop of Bayonne, was met on the International Bridge, closed for many years and which was opened for the passage of Our Lady of Fatima. In the middle of the bridge the two Bishops embraced before the statue passed. The applause and "vivas" resounded on all sides and the two contingents mingled fraternally under the eyes of their common Heavenly Mother.

Then the European Tour continued by Dax, Lourdes, Tarence, La Rochelle, Eure and Loir Somme, etc. On August 1st Our Lady of Fatima entered Belgium. It was a triumphal pilgrimage, travelling for five months through the different dioceses and almost all of the parishes which rivalled each other's fervour in receiving the heavenly "Missionary of God" as she was called.

At Maestricht (Holland) where Our Lady of Fatima went to preside at a Congress of Catholic Youth, the Protestants fraternised with Catholics to receive with the utmost possible solemnity the "Missionary of God."

After a detour through Luxembourg and Paris, Our Lady of Fatima arrived at Brussels where she was hailed with such indescribable enthusiasm that the clergy and the people kept her by force for several weeks, a real prisoner of their faith and love.

Pray that the frontiers and hearts of other nations open also, whilst there is yet time, to the heavenly Missionary of Fatima who comes to offer them lovingly the providential help of her Message, promising at the same time a christian and lasting peace, if the people would but welcome this Message and put it into practice.

The World-wide Tour

The great Message of Fatima is now known everywhere. It is no longer only from Europe but from every part of the world that His Lordship the Bishop of Fatima receives letters of goodwill begging him to send at once to their country the heavenly Messenger of God. It was during the Pilgrimage of November 13th, 1947, that five large statues were solemnly blessed at Fatima by five different bishops for this "World-wide Tour."

One of them was intended for Angola (W. Africa), another for the Philippine Islands, the third for Belgium, the fourth for China. The fifth was taken to North America on November 16th, 1947, accompanied with honour by several persons of rank. On the 19th it was solemnly received and crowned by Mgr. Vachon, Archbishop of Ottawa, in the presence of more than 50,000 faithful assembled in the University Stadium of the town. During the two months that Our Lady of Fatima travelled through the country in every direction, the fervour of the faithful rivalled the zeal of the clergy and hierarchy, who by pastoral letters had prepared their minds and hearts to receive the abundant graces which Our Lady of Fatima came to grant them.

On December 8th, 1947, Our Lady of Fatima passed on to the United States, where the bishops, assembled at Washington, approved of the "World-wide Tour" of the Virgin of Fatima and charged Mgr. O'Hara, Archbishop of Buffalo, with the work of organisation.

122

This visit of Our Lady of Fatima, officially arranged and organised by the bishops themselves, proceeded throughout the United States with a magnificence truly American. At Buffalo the immense cathedral was already packed and a file of faithful eight deep and about two miles long waited to get as near as possible to venerate the heavenly "Missionary from God."

CHAPTER XI

The Fiftieth Anniversary

On May 13th, 1967, fiftieth anniversary of the first Fatima apparition, the Holy Father Pope Paul VI made a visit to the Shrine.

Extensive preparations had been made for the Golden Jubilee, and a crowd estimated at one and a half millions came to the rugged Serra de Aire from Portugal and from the four corners of the globe for the celebrated occasion.

The visit of the Pope had ensured that the attention of the world's mass media would be focussed on Fatima.

The third and only survivor of the children who saw Our Lady, Sister Lucy of the Immaculate Heart of Mary O.D.C. was brought from the Carmelite cloister of Coimbra at the Pope's request, a request that was the equivalent of a command.

Sister Lucia knelt down beside the Pontiff for some time whilst the huge crowd burst into the singing of the famous Fatima "ave" and then cried out *"viva il Papa."*

The crowd began crying *"viva il Papa!"* once more when the Pope knelt beside the statue of Our Lady of Fatima, hung a rosary on it, and asked Our Lady's intercession for world peace.

Then the Pope called Sr. Lucy to the microphone and introduced her to the mighty assembly. The enthusiasm of the crowd was unbounded.

It was reported that at one point Sr. Lucy asked to speak privately with the Pope. The Holy Father is reported to have said *"As you see this is not the time"* and to have told her to communicate with him through her bishop.

The day's ceremonies consisted in an open air Mass celebrated by Pope Paul and a series of addresses by him. During the Mass he gave Communion to fifty people selected at random from the crowd.

The Pope indicated a deep concern for the present divisions in the Church, making his pilgrimage to supplicate Our Lady for peace in the Church and peace in the world.

"Think of the gravity and grandeur of this hour," the

Pontiff said, *"which can be decisive for the history of present and future generations."*

He urged that the counsels of prayer and penance which Our Lady gave us at Fatima be followed.

He begged us all to offer to our separated brethren *"our faith in its clearcut authenticity and its original beauty"* and warned the Church that delusion would follow any attempt to attain Christian unity by failing to do this.

"We want to ask of Mary," he said, *"a living Church, a true Church, a united Church, a holy Church."*

He had come as a pilgrim, he said, to offer, *"a filial homage to beseech Our Lady of Fatima, that She may bring about the reign of the inestimable blessing of peace in the Church and in the world."*

While he was at the Shrine the Pope prayed especially for *"those nations in which religious liberty is almost totally suppressed and where the negation of God is promulgated.*

"We pray for the faithful of these nations," he added *"that the intimate strength of God may sustain them and that true civil liberty be conceded to them once more."* He continued, *"This is the way to peace—through prayer."*

Another of the highlights of the Golden Jubilee was the chartered flight around the world—to twenty-one nations—by the Bishop of Leiria-Fatima and various Blue Army leaders during which the Bishop presented Pilgrim Virgin statues that had been blessed by the Pope to the national hierarchies of countries visited.

It would be impossible to enumerate the multitudes of ceremonies, demonstrations, and proclamations around the world honouring the Jubilee Year of the Fatima revelations.

In the following year the Blue Army, through its U.S. office, arranged for the Bishop of Leiria-Fatima to deliver Pilgrim Statues to the various nation States of Africa, and by 1969 a total of forty-three of the Statues had been delivered around the world. Finally forty-three jewelled crowns were delivered to the recipients of the Statues and a combined coronation was arranged for May 13th, 1971. A worldwide consecration of dioceses and nations took place on that day, Cardinal O'Boyle officiating in Washington, Cardinal Gilroy in Sydney, and Cardinal Renard of Lyons, France, at the Shrine of Fatima itself. Many Archbishops and Bishops also participated in various parts of the world.

Sadly, these events were only cursorily reported in the

Catholic press, and almost totally ignored by the mass media.

The message of Our Lady, representing truth and goodness, is hated by a corrupt world, rejected and despised as was the Messiah Himself.

This means that Fatima crusaders must work harder than ever, must make more sacrifices, must show great patience, forbearance and love to their blind fellow citizens; for the message of love must conquer and WILL conquer the perverse hearts of men, bringing about Russia's conversion and the great era of Christian peace and love that is to come.

CHAPTER XII

A World Influence

As we have seen, the tours of Our Lady of Fatima soon became European and finally world-wide, which is very consoling and full of promise. But it is important to understand it fully. It is not merely a question of travelling around the world to present a statue for the veneration of the faithful. This is not a mere statue: it is a message from heaven which the "World-wide Tour" of Our Lady of Fatima brings to the world for its salvation. The modern world which pretends to do without God is being punished for its sins. It is affected by a lack of balance inexplicable by natural reason; a kind of satanic malady which will lead it straight to ruin, material, moral and religious, if someone does not stop it in time. All the specialised treatments have been long and loyally tried; and all these human remedies have constantly and invariably proved powerless. Reason itself, disconcerted by such an epidemic of collective and contagious madness, is forced to consider the religious explanation and to diagnose a superhuman or preternatural evil which has its origin in the eruption of the sins of the world and in the Divine anger, and which only help from heaven can cure. The Message of Fatima constitutes exactly the supernatural help brought by Our Lady of Fatima to peoples whom she visits on her world-wide tours.

To receive, then, Our Lady of Fatima, is not to welcome an ordinary religious statue; it is to give explicit and public testimony to the fact that one wishes to accept with faith and gratitude the heavenly Message of Fatima, and faithfully to put it into practice, so as to share in the consoling promises of a Christian and lasting peace, the peace of Christ in the reign of Christ. That is the real meaning of world-wide tours of Our Lady of Fatima and of the welcome that is given her.

Certainly, one can assert that the Message of Fatima is not a Dogma of Faith, and that everyone is free to accept it or not. But one must be careful, because the actual calamities, without being an article of faith, are none the less a bitter reality which overwhelms us; and the use of freedom in the refusal of the help offered entails responsibility also.

Let us get back to the simplicity of children so recommended by Our Lord. The providential help which the Holy Virgin brings us in the Message of Fatima is not presented to us unsupported by solid proofs. It is supported from the beginning by the extraordinary marvels of 1917 and by many others of different kinds that followed. Moreover, the competent ecclesiastical authority has formally approved it after a deep searching canonical inquiry which lasted for many years.

Let us not credit ourselves with more prudence and reserve than all these competent authorities; let us accept with gratitude the help from heaven which Our Lady of Fatima brings us. Let us loyally welcome her Message and faithfully put it into practice; *but above all let us not delay in doing so.*

CHAPTER XIII

A Grave Message

In reply to certain questions of His Lordship the Bishop of Leiria, Lucy wrote on December 8th, 1941: "I add that the prayer and penance offered up in Portugal have not yet appeased the Divine Justice, because they have not been accompanied by a true contrition, and by the necessary amendment of life. I hope that Jacinta will intercede for us in heaven."

The Portuguese bishops, however, recognised frankly in their collective letter of 1942, all that their country has already done in response to the heavenly message of Fatima. Portugal, they admit, is no longer recognisable, so profound and extensive is the transformation effected in the country! If Portugal, that has already done so much, has not sufficiently understood what the Blessed Virgin expects of it, and is not secure from chastisement, what can be said of us? *Have we meditated sufficiently on the exceptional gravity of the situation of the world? Have we understood sufficiently clearly the serious nature of the heavenly message and the urgent necessity of giving it a sincere, immediate and wholehearted welcome?*

Let us reflect before God on these thoughts, and let us set to work immediately with holy ardour. Let us amend our lives. Let our conduct be openly and fully Christian. Let us banish mortal sin and even every deliberate venial sin from our souls. Let us recite the Rosary every day, and as far as possible with the family. Let us do penance, first for our own sins, and then for the sins of the world. Let us consecrate ourselves to the Immaculate Heart of Mary and adopt the practice of the First Saturdays of the month.

It is in our own interest that Our Lady of Fatima has made these requests; let us not neglect them. Instead of a military mobilisation, *it is a spiritual mobilisation that is required*. The situation is serious, we cannot hesitate. He who claims that he has not the time now to answer this Message of salvation should fear lest he may have, soon perhaps, to undergo the horrors of war, to see the ruin of his goods, of his family, and perhaps of his country!

But if we respond to the Message from heaven, and begin resolutely a new life, then, let us have confidence: in spite of all that we may still have to suffer, the Immaculate Heart of Mary will intercede with her Divine Son, and will help us to escape the terrible rigours of the Divine Justice, outraged by our sins.

Our Lady of the Rosary of Fatima, pray for us!

No better words can more fittingly conclude Fr. da Cruz's magnificent booklet than this Christmas exhortation of the beloved Pope of Peace, Pope Pius XII:

"The call of the moment is not for lamentation, but for action: not lamentation over what has been, but a building up of what is to arise. It is for the best and most distinguished members of the Christian family, filled with the enthusiasm of Crusaders, to unite in a spirit of truth, justice and love to the Cause. *God wills it!* They must be ready to serve, to sacrifice themselves like the Crusaders of old! The essential aim of this necessary and holy Crusade is that the *Star of Peace*, the Star of Bethlehem, may shine out again over the whole of mankind in all its brilliant splendour and reassuring consolation . . . *Fight for the cause of mankind!"*

"Let us go with confidence to the throne of grace . . ."

"Thou art the hope of the world . . . !"

APPENDIX

The Confraternity of the Rosary

We have seen the capital importance of the holy Rosary. A word may be added here on the *Confraternity of the Rosary,* which is one of the most efficacious means of spreading this devotion in parishes.

Its Origin: Established in the early days of the Rosary devotion, it was spread in the fifteenth century by Blessed Alain de la Roche who assures us that he received its statutes from the Blessed Virgin herself.

Its Great Advantages: The Confraternity of the Rosary offers its members the following immense advantages:

1. An altogether special protection of the Queen of Heaven. (See the Encyclical of Leo XIII of September 8th,. 1893).

2. A special participation during life, at the hour of death, and after death, in all the prayers, penances, and good works of the numerous members of this Confraternity, spread throughout the entire world. What a treasure of graces for the living and the dead!

3. A share in all the spiritual goods of the whole Dominican Order. What an immense capital! The good works of all the Saints and Beati of the Order: martyrs, confessors, virgins and holy women—over 300 in number! The merits of all the Masses offered to God each day by all the Friars Preachers: nearly 5,000 of them! Without speaking of the mortifications, watches, fasts, prayers, Communions of all the Fathers, Brothers, Sisters, Missionaries, and Tertiaries of the Order!

4. An immense treasure of indulgences granted to this Confraternity and applicable to the souls in Purgatory. The Rosary is "the Queen of indulgenced devotions,"

and the Confraternity of the Rosary is the richest Confraternity of indulgences. This is what led St. Alphonsus to say: "After Holy Mass the best means of relieving the souls in Purgatory is to join the Confraternity of the Rosary."

Its importance is capital in the eyes of the Saints and of the Sovereign Pontiffs.

Saint Charles Borromeo esteemed the Confraternity of the Rosary so highly that he ordered it to be erected in *all* the parishes of his large Archdiocese of Milan!

Saint Alphonsus de Liguori wrote on the utility of the Confraternity: "In the many missions I have preached, I have come to the conclusion that there are more sins in one single man who does not belong to the Confraternity of Mary than in twenty who do!"

The Holy Cure d'Ars said: "If anyone has the happiness of being in the Confraternity of the Rosary, he has, in all corners of the globe, brothers who pray for him." And he added: "For a member of the Confraternity of the Rosary to succeed in losing his soul, he would have do do himself as much violence as the other faithful do to save their souls, so abundant are the graces of this Confraternity!"

Leo XIII has insisted very much on the Confraternity of the Rosary, especially in the encyclicals "Laetitiae Sanctae" of 1893 and "Augustissimae Virginis" of 1897. "Among the different associations," he wrote, "We do not hesitate to give *the place of honour to the Confraternity of the Rosary*." And, after explaining how the Confraternity multiplies the benefits of the Rosary, the great Pope makes earnest appeals to priests and Bishops:

To Priests: "You ought," he said, "to apply yourselves with the greatest zeal to founding, developing and directing these Confraternities of the Rosary. This appeal is addressed not only to the sons of St. Dominic, for whom this is an important duty of their state, but to *all priests* who have the care of souls. It is also our earnest desire that missionaries, those who take the Gospel to pagan lands as well as those who

132

preach in Christian countries, give themselves with equal zeal to this activity." (Laetitiae Sanctae).

Its Facility: To join the Confraternity of the Rosary and to share in its immense advantages, it is sufficient:

(*a*) to have one's name inscribed on the Register of a Confraternity canonically erected in one's parish or elsewhere. Dominican Priories have traditionally sponsored this confraternity.

(*b*) to promise to recite, at least once a week, the *whole* Rosary, i.e., three Rosaries, while meditating on the Fifteen Mysteries. This promise is not a vow and does not bind under pain of sin, except that those who are not habitually faithful to it are deprived of the immense spiritual goods and indulgences of the Confraternity. The three Rosaries and even the individual decades may be separated.

A practical manner of doing it is to recite two decades on week days and three on Sundays, *meditating successively on the Fifteen Mysteries*. In this way the three Rosaries are said in the week, which is the minimum required to gain the spiritual favours of the Confraternity of the Rosary. Happy are those who can do more!

And you who already recite your Rosary daily, *have your name inscribed in the Confraternity of the Rosary without delay,* for without any additional obligation, you will share in all the spiritual treasures of this rich Confraternity. What a pity to deprive yourself of them!

No subscription is required either for inscription or afterwards. Therefore there is no pecuniary expense for the poor or for the parish.

Furthermore, the Confraternity of the Rosary does not involve any external interference in the parish, for it is a parochial work, *entirely under the control of the Pastor who is always the Director*. In parishes where there are several districts to be served, it forms a centre of prayer in each. It renders invaluable service in grouping the faithful and maintaining the parochial spirit, especially on a Sunday, if on this day Mass cannot be celebrated there.

What an advantage it is for a parish to have this Confraternity to keep it living and active, and to spread among the faithful the love of the holy Rosary, so earnestly demanded by the Blessed Virgin as a remedy of divine efficacy for present-day evils, and which according to Pius XI *"will save the world!"*

Act of Consecration of Pope Pius XII

QUEEN of the Most Holy Rosary, Help of Christians, Refuge of the Human Race, Conqueror in all God's battles, we humbly prostrate ourselves before Thy throne, confident that we shall receive mercy, grace, bountiful assistance and protection in the present calamity, not through our own inadequate merits, but solely through the great goodness of Thy Maternal Heart.

To thee, to thy Immaculate Heart in this, humanity's tragic hour, we consign and consecrate ourselves in union, not only with the Mystical Body of thy Son Jesus, Holy Mother Church, now in such suffering and agony in so many places and sorely tried in so many ways, but also with the entire world, torn by fierce strife, consumed in a fire of hate, victim of its own wickedness.

May the sight of such widespread material and moral destruction, of the sorrows and anguish of countless fathers and mothers, husbands and wives, brothers and sisters, and innocent children, of the great number of lives cut off in the flower of youth, of bodies mangled in horrid slaughter, and of tortured and agonized souls in danger of being lost eternally, move thee to compassion for our wretched plight.

O Mother of Mercy, obtain peace for us from God, and above all procure for us those graces which prepare, establish and assure that peace! Queen of Peace, pray for us and give to the world now at war the peace for which all peoples yearn, peace in the truth, the justice and the charity of Christ. Give peace to the warring nations and to the souls of men, that in the tranquillity of order the Kingdom of God may at length prevail.

Extend thy protection to infidels also and to all those who are still in the shadow of death; give them peace and grant that on them, too, may shine the sun of truth, that they may unite with us in proclaiming before the One and Only Saviour of the world "Glory be to God in the Highest and on earth peace to men of good will!" (Luke II, 14).

Give peace to the peoples separated by error or by discord, and in particular to those who profess such singular devotion to thee and in whose homes thy venerated image always found an honoured place, although it may now rest concealed until the coming of a happier day; bring them back to the One True Fold of Christ, under the One True Shepherd.

Obtain peace and complete freedom for the Holy Church of God; stay the spreading flood of modern paganism; enkindle in the faithful the love of purity, the practice of the Christian life and an apostolic zeal, so that the servants of God may be multiplied in merit and in number.

Lastly, as the Church and the entire human race were consecrated to the Sacred Heart of Jesus, so that, in reposing all their hope in Him He might become for them the sign and pledge of victory and salvation; so we in like manner, consecrate ourselves for ever also to thee and to thy Immaculate Heart, Our Mother, Queen of the World, that thy love and patronage may hasten the triumph of the Kingdom of God, and that all nations, at peace with one another and with God, may proclaim thee Blessed and with thee may raise their voices to resound from pole to pole in the chant of the everlasting Magnificat of glory, love and gratitude to the Heart of Jesus, where alone they can find truth and life and peace. Amen.

The Memorare

Remember, O most gracious virgin Mary, that never was it known that anyone who fled to your protection, implored your help or sought your intercession was left unaided. Inspired with this confidence I fly unto you, O virgin of virgins my Mother. To you do I come, before you I stand sinful and sorrowful. O Mother of the Word Incarnate despise not my petitions but in your mercy hear and answer me. Amen.

How To Say The Rosary

The whole Rosary is composed of fifteen decades; each decade is recited in honour of a mystery of the life of Our Lord and His Blessed Mother, beginning with the *annunciation* of the Incarnation and ending with Mary's triumphal *coronation* in heaven. A decade consists of one *Our Father*, ten *Hail Marys*, a *Glory be to the Father* and the prayer Our Lady of Fatima asked the Fatima children to add after each decade: the *Decade Prayer*. The ordinary beads or chaplets contain five decades. It is customary to recite five decades at a time while meditating on one set of mysteries.

The Hail Mary

The angelic salutation is so heavenly and so beyond us in its depth of meaning that Blessed Alan de la Roche held that no mere creature could ever possibly understand it, and that only Our Lord and Saviour Jesus Christ who was born of the Blessed Virgin can really explain it.

The angelic salutation is a most concise summary of all that Catholic theology teaches about the Blessed Virgin. It is divided into two parts, that of praise and petition: the first shows all that goes to make up Mary's greatness and the second all that we need to ask her for and that we may expect to receive through her goodness.

The greatest event in the whole history of the world was the Incarnation of the Eternal Word by whom the world was redeemed and peace was restored between God and men. Our Lady was chosen as his instrument for this tremendous event and it was put into effect when she was greeted with the angelic salutation. The Archangel Gabriel, one of the leading princes of the heavenly court, was chosen as ambassador to bear these glad tidings.

She also taught it to Blessed Alan de la Roche and said to him in a vision: "When people say one hundred and fifty Angelic Salutations this prayer is very helpful to them and is

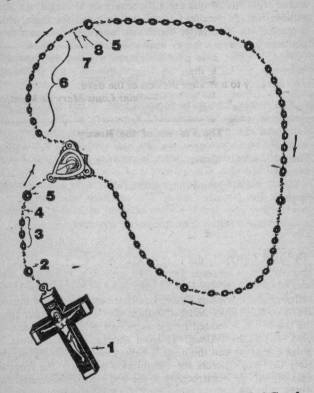

1. Make the sign of the Cross and say the **Apostles' Creed.**
2. Say the **Our Father.**
3. Say three **Hail Marys.**
4. Say the **Glory be to the Father.**
5. Announce the Mystery; then say the **Our Father.**
6. Say ten **Hail Marys,** while meditating on the Mystery.
7. Say the **Glory be to the Father.**
8. Say the **Fatima Decade Prayer.**

a very pleasing tribute to me. *But they will do better still and will please me even more if they say these salutations while meditating on the life, death and passion of Jesus Christ—for this meditation is the soul of this prayer.*"

For, in reality, the Rosary said without meditating on the sacred mysteries of our salvation would be almost like a body without a soul: excellent matter but without the form which is meditation—this latter being that which sets it apart from all other devotions.

To think that it is possible to say prayers that are finer and more beautiful than the Our Father and the Hail Mary is to fall prey to a strange illusion of the devil.

—Saint Louis Mary de Montfort

The Prayers of the Rosary

The Sign of the Cross

In the name of the Father and of the Son and of the Holy Spirit, Amen.

The Apostles' Creed

I believe in God, the Father Almighty, Creator of heaven and earth; and in Jesus Christ, His only Son, our Lord: who was conceived of the Holy Spirit, born of the Virgin Mary, suffered under Pontius Pilate, was crucified: dead, and buried. He descended into hell;* the third day he rose again from the dead: He ascended into heaven, sits at the right hand of God, the Father Almighty; from thence He shall come to judge the living and the dead. I believe in the Holy Spirit, the Holy Catholic Church, the communion of Saints, the forgiveness of sins, the resurrection of the body, and life everlasting. Amen.

The Our Father

Our Father, Who art in heaven hallowed be Thy name; Thy kingdom come; Thy will be done on earth as it is in

* The word hell means here the state or place where the souls of the just who died before Christ waited for the redemption.

heaven. Give us this day our daily bread; and forgive us our trespasses as we forgive them who trespass against us: and lead us not into temptation, but deliver us from evil. Amen.

The Hail Mary

Hail Mary, full of grace! the Lord is with thee: blessed art thou amongst women, and blessed is the fruit of thy womb, Jesus. Holy Mary, Mother of God, pray for us sinners, now and at the hour of our death. Amen.

The Glory Be to the Father

Glory be to the Father, and to the Son and to the Holy Spirit. As it was in the beginning, is now, and ever shall be, world without end. Amen.

The Fatima Decade Prayer

O my Jesus, forgive us our sins, save us from the fire of hell, and bring all souls to heaven, especially those who most need your mercy.

The Hail Holy Queen

Hail, Holy Queen, Mother of mercy, hail, our life, our sweetness, and our hope! To thee do we cry, poor banished children of Eve! To thee do we send up our sighs, mourning and weeping in this valley of tears! Turn then, most gracious advocate, thine eyes of mercy towards us; and after this, our exile, show unto us the blessed fruit of thy womb, Jesus! O clement, O loving, O sweet Virgin Mary!

Pray for us O Holy Mother of God. That we may be made worthy of the promises of Christ.

The Five Joyful Mysteries

1. The Annunciation.
2. The Visitation.
3. The Birth of Jesus.

4. The Presentation.
5. The Finding of the Child Jesus in the Temple.

The Five Sorrowful Mysteries

6. The Agony in the Garden.
7. The Scourging at the Pillar.
8. The Crowning with Thorns.
9. The Carrying of the Cross.
10. The Crucifixion.

The Five Glorious Mysteries

11. The Resurrection.
12. The Ascension.
13. The Descent of the Holy Spirit.
14. The Assumption.
15. The Crowning of the Blessed Virgin.

HEAVEN'S THREE POINT PLAN FOR THE SPIRITUAL AND TEMPORAL SALVATION OF MANKIND IN OUR CENTURY

Revealed by OUR BLESSED MOTHER in 1917

"If my wishes are fulfilled . . . . there will be peace."

HEAVEN'S THREE POINT PLAN

1. Prayer—Daily Rosary
"I am the Lady of the Rosary. You must say the Rosary every day, and say it properly."

2. Penance and Reparation
"People must amend their lives and ask pardon for their sins. They must no longer offend Our Lord, who is already offended too much."

"The sacrifice required of every person is *the fulfilment of the duties of his state in life and the observance of God's law.*" "Further, I request Holy Communion of Reparation on the first Saturday of each month."

3. Devotion and Consecration to the Immaculate Heart of Mary

"The Lord wishes to establish in the world Devotion to my Immaculate Heart. I promise salvation to those who embrace it."

ACT OF CONSECRATION TO THE IMMACULATE HEART OF MARY

O Immaculate Heart of Mary, Queen of Heaven and Earth, and tender Mother of men, in accordance with thy ardent wish made known at Fatima, I consecrate to thee myself, my brethren, my country, and the whole human race.

Reign over us and teach us how to make the Heart of Jesus reign and triumph in us, and around us, as It has reigned and triumphed in thee.

Reign over us, dearest Mother, that we may be thine in prosperity and in adversity, in joy and in sorrow, in health and in sickness, in life and in death.

O most compassionate Heart of Mary, Queen of Virgins, watch over our minds and hearts and preserve them from the deluge of impurity which thou didst lament so sorrowfully at Fatima. We want to be pure like thee. We want to atone for the many crimes committed against Jesus and thee. We want to call down upon our country and the whole world the peace of God in justice and charity.

Therefore, we now promise to imitate thy virtues by the practice of a Christian life without regard to human respect.

We resolve to receive Holy Communion regularly and to offer thee five decades of the Rosary each day, together with our sacrifices, in the spirit of reparation and penance. Amen.

I Pledge Myself to Our Lady

Dear Queen and Mother, who promised at Fatima to convert Russia and bring peace to all mankind, in reparation to your Immaculate Heart for my sins and the sins of the whole world, I solemnly promise:

1) To offer up every day the sacrifices demanded by my daily duty;

2) To say part of the Rosary daily while meditating on the Mysteries;

3) To wear the Scapular of Mt. Carmel as profession of this promise and as an act of consecration to you. I shall renew this promise often, especially in moments of temptation.

Prayer of the Angel who prepared the children for the apparitions

Bowing down his forehead to the ground, the angel said:

"My God, I believe in Thee, I adore Thee, I hope in Thee, and I love Thee. I ask pardon for those who do not believe, who do not adore, who do not hope, and who do not love Thee."

"Most Holy Trinity, Father, Son and Holy Spirit I adore You profoundly and offer the Most Precious Body, Blood, Soul and Divinity of Our Lord Jesus Christ present in all the Tabernacles of the world, in reparation for the outrages by which He is Himself offended."

"By the Infinite merits of His Sacred Heart and by the intercession of the Immaculate Heart of Mary, I beg of You the conversion of sinners."

Formula of Offering

O Jesus, it is for love of You, for the conversion of sinners, for the Holy Father, and in reparation for the sins committed against the Immaculate Heart of Mary.

May 13:	"Say the Rosary **every day to obtain peace** for the world."
June 13:	"I want you to say the Rosary **every day.**"
July 13:	"I want you to continue to say the Rosary **every**
Aug. 19:	day in honour of Our Lady of the Rosary."
	"I want you to continue to say the Rosary **every day.**"
Sept 13:	"Continue to say the Rosary."
Oct. 13:	"I want to tell you that **I am Our Lady of the Rosary;** continue to say the Rosary **every day.**"

PRAYER TO ST. JOSEPH

(St. Joseph is the only Saint, besides Our Lady, who appeared at Fatima, Portugal, in 1917 when the world was warned that, "Russia will spread her errors throughout the world . . ." unless mankind fulfilled certain requests for prayers and penance.

At Fatima, St. Joseph appeared holding the Child Jesus in his arms and he blessed three times the more than 70,000 people gathered there. It is of him that it has been said: "The sound of victory will be heard when the faithful recognise the sanctity of St. Joseph.")

Tender-hearted Father, faithful guardian of Jesus, chaste spouse of the Mother of God, model of all who labor, lover of poverty, glory of family life, solace of the afflicted, hope of the sick, patron of the dying, terror of demons, protector of the Holy Church.

To thee, O Blessed Joseph, we have recourse in our tribulations, and while imploring the aid of thy most holy Spouse, we also confidently invoke thy patronage.

Appease the Divine anger so justly inflamed by our crimes; beg of Jesus mercy for thy children. Amid the splendors of eternity, forget not the sorrows of those who suffer, those who pray, those who weep; stay the Almighty Arm which smites us, that by thy prayers and those of thy most Holy Spouse, the Heart of Jesus may be moved to pity and to pardon.

As thou did once rescue the Child Jesus from imminent peril to His life, so now defend the Holy Church of God from the snares of her enemies and from all adversity. Shield each one of us with unceasing patronage, that imitating thy example, and supported by thy aid, we may be enabled to live a good life, die a holy death, and secure everlasting happiness in heaven. Amen.